Woman ...
Man's Best Friend

by
BRUCE MICHAELS

*A good man understands that a woman is not a possession ...
But a compliment, and most beautiful when permitted to be
"ALL" that she can be.*

Published by Love Is Forever, LLC
Cleveland, Ohio

Copyright © 2010, Love Is Forever, LLC

ISBN 978-0-9801574-0-6
LCCN 2010939597

All rights reserved. No parts of this publication may be reproduced, stored in a retrieval system or transmitted, in any form or by any means electronic, mechanical, photocopying, recorded or otherwise, without the written prior permission of the author.

My Dedication ...

Special thanks to "The Lord" for always being there for me.

I dedicate this book to my parents for showing me how they have shared a wonderful 62-year marriage. To all my relatives, past and present, who taught me the power of a hug, a kind word, and love.

To Susan, without you believing in me, I would never have thought outside of the box of life and considered doing anything out of the ordinary, like write a book. When I had my doubts, you were always there for me, supporting me with encouragement. You opened my mind and heart with tender love. You made it possible for me "To Dream the Impossible" and "Keeping My Dream Alive". You will always have a special place in my heart. Thank you for all your support and Love.

Special Acknowledgments

Thank you for your help, encouragement and input:

Peter Benea
Luckey B
Joyce
George M
Yvette

Woman ...
Man's Best Friend

by
BRUCE MICHAELS

Contents

Preface: What men need to learn — xi

Introduction — xiii
    This book is geared toward men to help them understand the importance of being best friends with their partners — xiv

My Story: An Average Man's Journey to Lasting Friendship — xix
    My Revelation — xxi

Chapter One: Bad Apples — 1

Chapter Two: Qualities of a Good Man — 5
    Real Life Observations — 10
    A Thread of Hope — 13
    The Forgotten Phone Call — 14

Chapter Three: Self-Assessment — 19
    Do You Play Golf? — 19
    What Type of Man Are YOU? — 20
    Assessing Your Personal Characteristic Traits — 21
    The Results — 22
    Communication — 23
    Solving Communication Problems — 26
    R-E-S-P-E-C-T — 27

Real-Life Outtake 29
Recognizing Pitfalls 30

Chapter Four: Analyzing the Health of Your Relationship   35
Identifying Problems Within Your Relationship 35
A True Man Will Learn to Control His Temper 37
The Fine Art of Compromise 39
Listening: It Takes Two 39
Keeping a Scorecard: The Kiss of Death 40
Ego 41
Venting 42
Nagging 42
Negative Attitude 43
Jealousy 43
Bar-Room Chatter 44
I Need My Space 45
Trust 45
Faithfulness 45
Cheating 46

Chapter Five: Friendship—The Foundation of a Healthy Relationship   51
The Components of Being a Friend 52
The Daily Routine: Strengthening Your Friendship 55
Defining Couples and Boundaries 56
Making Your Partner Feel Important 57

Chapter Six: Make a Plan to Improve Yourself   61
Are You Ready to Change? 61
What Type of Person Do You Want to Become? 62
Open Discussion: What type of person do you want to be? 64
Negative Patterns 65
Day-to-Day Actions Make a Difference 66
Defining Your Goals 67

Contents ix

    A Plan for Action   69
    This is a *Team Effort*   70
    What's Most Important is Forward Movement   71

Chapter Seven: Improving Your Lasting Relationship   73
    Staying on the Tightrope   73
    Setting Priorities and Realistic Expectations   74
    Increasing Your Emotional Connection   74
    The Simple Act of Being Together   74
    Continually Developing Your Relationship   80
    Strengths Over Weaknesses   84
    Find the Solution or Compromise Together   85
    She's Special—So Remind Her   85

Chapter Eight: The Importance of Physical Contact   89
    Intimacy in Your Relationship   90
    Physical Affection   90
    Embrace: The Power of a Hug   91
    The Art of the Kiss   91
    A Little Cuddle Time   92
    Massaging Out the Kinks   93
    Foreplay vs. Sex   93
    Appreciation as a Form of Intimacy   94
    Create a Keepsake Box   95
    Take a Cruise Ship Excursion   95

Conclusion: My Last Bit of Advice   97
    Tune Up Your Relationship   97

Bonus Section: Women Love Poetry   101
    Romance Is ...   102

Afterthought   104

Preface

What men need to learn

Love can be complicated. All relationships take work. They need to be attended to, nurtured and invested in. It's easy to fall prey to ignoring relationships, often without realizing it—wondering what went wrong, why your relationship has failed, spun out of control, crumbled, or lost its romance.

If you talk to people who are in healthy relationships you will discover they all have one thing in common: *friendship*. They develop a strong friendship from the beginning, and still have to work at it from time to time. The secret is to remember how and why you fell "in love."

People in healthy relationships remember to cherish the moments they have together, not allowing the confusion in life to get the best of them. They know exactly where to put their efforts and are willing to put forth the extra effort. They realize the importance of being their partner's best friend and the long term benefits.

Through the eyes of your average Joe, I want to share with you what I have learned through the years and believe are the beneficial principles of creating and sustaining a strong, enduring, loving, romantically enhanced relationship... forever and a day.

In this book you will learn to develop the patience and skills for being ...

                      Best Friends

Introduction

Woman ... Man's Best Friend is designed to give couples of all ages the tools they need to make their relationship more fulfilling, fun, passionate, and exciting, regardless of the type of relationship they are in. It is a self-help guide for everyone, no matter if you are single, divorced, remarried, empty nesters, or newlyweds.

A good relationship requires love, honesty, understanding, sharing, giving, respect, and togetherness with a bit of individual time mixed as well. No relationship is without disagreements, so it is important that you both are able to talk about anything that may be bothering you.

Within the pages of this book you'll find the following information:

- Why a base of friendship is the strongest foundation you can build with your partner and how to build this foundation one brick at a time.
- Why communication is the most important tool you have at your disposal, and how to ease the communication struggles many couples face.
- Why self-assessment is so critical before starting any process of change and how to honestly see where you're at in the process.

- Why goal setting is an essential part of making a plan for change and how both people within a relationship need to be stakeholders.
- How to take everything you've learned and together create a plan for change that you can stick to so your relationship can flourish.

I'm just your "average Bruce" and every point made in this book is based on my own personal experiences. With the help of one special woman, along with friends and acquaintances, I've learned the true meaning of friendship. I want to share how I have learned self-awareness and help you began the process of personal growth. Through a simple, caring, straightforward approach, my goal is to help you rekindle the flame of passion so your relationship can withstand the daily struggles that come your way.

This book is intended to be useful and enlightening. Through self-awareness, communication, and the continual self-improvement process you will learn not only what behaviors you demonstrate as a partner, but also how to develop the ability to change and become a better man.

While this book talks mainly to men, it's not meant for men only. Just as a relationship needs two people working at it daily to thrive, this book is designed to have *both* partners participate. In fact, throughout this book, you'll find stories and exercises for both partners to share and learn from.

The goals of this book are to help men:

- Establish and appreciate a strong foundation of friendship with their partner.
- Grow closer with their partner.
- Communicate more effectively and considerately.
- Become more aware of their actions and inactions and how they affect the outcome of their relationship.
- Learn to be a friend with their partner *for a lifetime*.

Introduction

I believe I've discovered what it takes to create a bond of equality, respect and love with a partner and how to grow in a long-term relationship. The benefits I have reaped are magically rich and I want to share what I have learned with you.

What comes to mind when you hear the phrase, "Man's best friend"? If you're like most people, the answer is a dog. And really, it's not such a bad answer. After all, dogs are loving, loyal, and attentive. They possess the exact traits you'd like to have in your partner, minus some obvious drooling drawbacks.

On the other end of the spectrum is the phrase, "In the doghouse," most often used when a man is in trouble with his partner. So on one hand, we have a dog being man's best friend, and on the other we have a guy out in the doghouse when he upsets his significant other in some form or fashion.

Confusing? The real question should be: "Why isn't the *man's partner* his best friend?" Why doesn't man see the rewards of being best friends with his partner? Makes you think, doesn't it? My search for that understanding is what led me to write this book for all the men who, like me at one point or another, didn't appreciate or realize the level of effort and commitment required to keep the love alive with their significant other. But once I started learning to become my partner's best friend I felt the rewards instantly. She became sweeter, kinder, sexier and more fun to be around, and love-making rose to a higher level.

There are an alarming number of couples who do not get along with one another. We like to think of falling in love as a fairytale, which it definitely can be, but achieving the happily ever after is another story altogether. What often starts out as a fairytale ends in disaster with couples walking away from each other, never really understanding what went wrong.

I'm sure you've heard many stories of bad relationships from friends, coworkers, family, and acquaintances. In all likelihood, you can immediately think of many couples within your circle of friends who have divorced or separated over the past year. The divorce rates in our country prove this claim.

Data taken from a study done in 2005 shows the following statistics:

Age at marriage for those who divorce in America:		
AGE	WOMEN	MEN
Under 20 years old	27.6%	11.7%
20 to 24 years old	36.6%	38.8%
25 to 29 years old	16.4%	22.3%
30 to 34 years old	8.5%	11.6%
35 to 39 years old	5.1%	6.5%

Source: www.divorcerate.org

Within the United States, the divorce rate is approximately 50 percent for first marriages, 67 percent for second marriages, and 74 percent for third marriages. The Americans for Divorce Reform estimate that **"Probably 40 or even possibly 50 percent of marriages will end in divorce if current trends continue."**

That last sentence, "if current trends continue" concerns me the most. What are these current trends? It is my opinion, the two contributing factors are:

1. **A couple's inability to communicate with each other in a meaningful manner.**
2. **A solid foundation of friendship within their relationship was never established.**

Conflicts of interest or disputes often lead to arguing, yelling, and eventually divorce. Unfortunately it seems to come easier than sensibly talking through the issues. In addition, it seems that many couples lack the depth of feeling that creates an indestructible bond between them. Wouldn't it help if couples were better friends? The answer to this question is an unequivocal **Yes!**

Unfortunately, the majority of the blame for these communication struggles primarily falls on the man—not because he is intentionally trying to sabotage his happiness, but because he has been programmed, through a variety of experiences and influences, to behave the way he does. Think about how married men are portrayed in movies and TV shows such as *According to Jim* and *King of Queens*. The husbands are portrayed as totally dysfunctional in their relationships. They sit in their chairs eating and drinking beer while their partner runs around taking care of the home and kids. Very seldom do you see the man helping out around the house, cleaning, doing the dishes, or taking care of his kids, thus putting the entire burden on the woman. Instead, what you see are men constantly trying to manipulate their partner. The message we as a society are sending is that it is normal and acceptable to behave this way.

Our culture polarizes the roles of men and women. Could this be one of the reasons for the increasing number of couples who are having difficulty relating to each other? I think it's a very strong possibility.

Men need to know that it is not only okay to be respectful, tender, kindhearted, and gentle all of the time, but necessary in order to have a healthy and wonderful relationship. Men need to learn how to be their partner's friend, to understand how important it is to fulfill their physical and emotional needs and the rewards that will follow.

My Story:
An Average Man's Journey to Lasting Friendship

"All, everything that I understand, I understand only because I love."

Leo Tolstoy

Ah. Love. It's everywhere, isn't it? Poems, novels, movies, and plays are written about it. Holidays are centered around it. We've all felt that first blush of love with someone, that giddy time when everything is right with the world and all we want to do is spend time with this new person in our life.

Unfortunately, reality sets in all too often when the giddiness gives way to miscommunication, arguments, snide remarks, and eventually ... the breakup. After the breakup, men seem confused, while most women have a good idea what went wrong.

While it's true that a successful relationship takes two people working at it together, women tend to be more perceptive and intuitive. They are not afraid to look at themselves, see what went wrong, and take the necessary steps to change (grow) so as not to repeat the same mistakes in their next relationship.

Men, on the other hand, don't usually see or care what went wrong and/or tend to blame others because they are unable to grasp an important basic concept of what makes a relationship successful: **Friendship.** We put our best foot forward for only a brief period of time, only to settle into a comfort zone. So we go on, never being aware of our issues, consistently making the same mistakes, over and over, relationship after relationship.

I know this all too well because it has happened to me. I was that man, the Average Joe, or in my case, the Average Bruce, until I met Susan.

Finding love isn't always difficult. It's all around us. The difficult part is keeping that love alive, and seeing it grow and mature into a lasting, fulfilling relationship. I know how difficult this is, but I promise you, it is doable.

Throughout the following pages, I'm going to ask you to:

- look at yourself;
- look at your partner;
- open yourself to the possibility of change; and
- make those changes one step at a time.

I'm going to share with you a story so you can see how these points changed my life and my relationship with Susan. I wouldn't be the man I am today if it wasn't for her.

Before I met Susan, my views about relationships were pretty much like most men: controlling and dominating toward their partners. I thought it was important to control my partner's thinking or opinions and to let my ego get in the way of proper judgment. I didn't understand how important it was to treat my partner like my best friend. Though, perhaps not *completely* typical, I mean, I was a nice guy and a gentlemen, but I wasn't aware of what it took to be a consistent friend. There were times I would look back at my past relationships and see some of my shortcomings—the things I did that contributed to my failures, but I didn't understand *how* to change those shortcomings.

Then when Susan came into my life, she opened my eyes to a more caring and thoughtful man.

My Story: An Average Man's Journey to Lasting Friendship

Our first date was amazing. We went to a romantic Italian restaurant with white tablecloths and candles. She was the most beautiful woman in the room. We were so comfortable together. We smiled and laughed all through dinner. Time had a way of standing still for us that evening and it felt like we were the only ones in the room. I was amazed how positive she was about life and her future, and at peace with who she was and the world around her. She had an incredible inner strength and I found myself in tune with her. As we talked throughout the evening our connection grew stronger with each word and each smile.

Our first kiss was electrifying and took my breath away. When we held hands it seemed to ignite our sleeping hearts. The more time I spent with Susan I felt as if I had stepped into a fairytale.

> *Our Love is a beautiful miracle in the making.*

Susan has taught me ...

- the true meaning of being best friends in a relationship;
- the importance of two people working together as a couple.
- how to look at people and see the good in them;
- to be more patient and not to sweat the little things; and
- how to be more patient in this crazy world, while staying happy.

My Revelation

One night, we had a conversation about relationships between men and women and she shared with me the story of her marriage, which had ended in divorce.

She said that her ex-husband was always too busy with work to participate in most family functions, leaving the responsibility to her to raise the children and take care of the house. Never feeling the support she needed from him, she tried to communicate with him as time went on, but he didn't seem to understand there was an issue and he didn't want to make any changes to their lifestyle, let alone their relationship. Even though she worked hard to fix the gaping holes in their marriage, they grew apart. Giving hugs, kisses, or even saying "I love you," became a thing of the past.

As I listened to Susan talk about the breakdown of her marriage, I began to realize how critical friendship is in a relationship. It really hit me that this woman was sharing a deep and private moment from her life, and it blew me away. It was the type of conversation that I'd have with a friend.

> *"I tried to explain to him what I needed. That I wanted him to understand the importance of making changes," she said to me.*

I'd never before experienced such a conversation with a woman. Her compassion was infectious, her insight accurate, and everything she said resonated inside of me.

This conversation changed my life. Everything we discussed that night made me rethink how men and woman communicate and how they relate to one another. It made me realize how miscommunication can create a gap so wide, that couples stop relating to each other altogether. Then she gave me a compliment that inspires me to this day:

> *"Bruce, you effortlessly use your instincts to do everything I want and need," she revealed.*

Susan went on to share how surprised she was that I was willing to listen and communicate my feelings to her. She appreciated how I tried to be aware of my actions and their consequences. She shared that she knew very few men who could communication effectively, much less give any thought to wanting to grow in a relationship. She said I was one of the very few men who believed that friendship was critical to a long-term commitment.

My Story: An Average Man's Journey to Lasting Friendship

With Susan's kind, patient ways, the foundation for this book was formed. She encouraged me to write it as sort of a guide to help men understand why friendship is important and how to achieve it in a relationship.

Though I didn't realize it at the time, as our relationship grew, so did our *friendship*.

Over the course of our relationship, I have learned many things I didn't know before:

- How to be a gentler man and how to love the one I'm with.
- To listen and communicate my feelings.
- How to be less critical, and why that is important.
- Relationships have boundaries that shouldn't be crossed during times of dispute.
- Saying "I'm sorry" and meaning it.
- How important it is to have a sense of humor.
- How to check my ego at the door.
- Understanding the importance of knowing your partner.
- Identifying your partner's shortcomings and not making them a big deal.
- Friendship is the foundation of all great relationships.

I learned all these things by really caring and paying attention, by discussing our concerns, and by setting aside my defenses and really listening to what Susan was saying. When I am out of line, I want her to tell me so. That is the only way I can learn to be a better partner. She does so in a kind, sensitive, and intelligent way. She is truly committed to making *us* a better couple.

There were times when she pointed things out to me and I became offended, but through her insight, I began to see and understand what she was saying—that it isn't important to win every battle, that it is okay to disagree, and that being in a healthy relationship takes time, patience, and the willingness to work hard at it every single day.

I truly believe that had I learned earlier in my life what I know now, I might have been able to change the outcome of my past relationships. Even so, upon looking back, there are many lessons I learned from each of those relationships, all of which have led me to the man I am today.

As you begin to make these changes you may find yourself feeling vulnerable, and that's okay. When I first met Susan, I put my heart on the line. I told her, "Here is my beating heart and I trust you with it." I can vouch that it's a good thing to feel vulnerable with the one you love. Vulnerability is a great character builder. So don't let it interfere with the process. Instead, learn and grow from it.

Susan is the inspiration as well as the instructor for this book. I am only the subscriber. Even today, long after our first fairytale meeting, my heart still races when I am around her and I am still amazed by who she is. For me, this journey has a happy ending, and it begins and ends with Susan.

If you have read this far, congratulations! Pour yourself a glass of wine for you and your partner, and enjoy this journey together. You'll find it energizing, thought provoking, and at the end, you'll have the best foundation of all: friendship.

I BELIEVE

I believe in the mystery of life
The miracles life brings
And the magic of a new day
I believe in angels, natural wonders
And the beauty inside people
I believe in rainbows, happy endings
And dreams that come true
I believe in sunshine
A bright shiny tomorrow
I believe in Love at first sight,
Fairy tales and their magic
But most of all
I believe in the power of LOVE
And
I believe in Love lasting a Lifetime

1 | Bad Apples

"Men are all alike—except the one you've met who's different."
                                                            Mae West

Every woman seems to have dated at least one, if not many, "bad apples," and they all have the stories to prove it. But what exactly is a bad apple in terms of a relationship? Bad apples are men who:

- Ignore the needs of their partners.
- Are more interested in the conquest than winning a woman's heart.
- Repeatedly break their promises.
- Are uncommunicative. (Women are looking for the silent type.)
- Don't tell the truth.
- Don't show affection.
- Keep late hours.
- Are more concerned with themselves and their own interests than they are learning about their partner's.

I'm not saying a man has to be perfect to not be dubbed a bad apple. No one is perfect. But when one man has too many bad apple traits, he ends up in one failed relationship after another.

Unfortunately, because many men today don't understand what it takes to make a relationship last and be successful, many women have had bad apple experiences. These experiences don't seem to be specific to a certain type of woman. Women of every age, race, size, shape, height, and hair color have had at least one bad experience. Not everyone you meet and date is the right match, but the pertinent issues are those that develop when a woman is involved with a bad apple.

> **How to avoid being a bad apple:**
> 1. Ask about her day.
> 2. Focus on *her* when she's talking to you.
> 3. Show some physical affection. Holding hands, hugs, back rubs, telling her you're thinking about her.

Today, an increasing number of women seem to be more reluctant than ever to get involved in a relationship. They're tired of men who won't open up and listen so as to become true partners. So, many women have simply thrown their hands up in defeat. Instead they would rather go out with their friends, and give up dating altogether.

I wish these were isolated incidents, but they appear to be growing ever more common. Too many single women have more than one unhappy story to tell about the misbehavior of men whom they have been involved with. Women have a difficult time trusting again and are hesitant to give love another chance, because they were hurt and/or taken advantage of. For this reason, women say it is easier to stay single than to have their hearts broken again, and who can blame them?

If you look at today's relationships, you'll see a dramatic difference from the relationships of yesteryear. People seem to put their own personal agenda ahead of their relationships, choosing instead to live in their own little 'it-is-all-about-me' world. This is the first sign of a serious disconnect within relationships, and many bad apples don't even realize they're doing it.

By learning to be your partner's friend, you can avoid the pitfalls of complacency, lack of communication, getting into a rut, and eventually drifting apart. Those actions will suffocate any relationship and throw it into an out-of-control spin. If you can have a real friendship with your partner, you have a good shot of making it work.

Now you're probably thinking, "Seriously, why would I want to be friends with my partner?" It's simple, although there's a lot more to it. We all know what friendship is. Where some men go astray is in thinking that friendship is the relationship they have with only their buddies, so there is no need to establish friendship with their partner. Both of these ideas are flawed.

Friendship with a woman is different than friendship with a man, but is crucial to the success of your relationship, though some elements of both types of friendships are the same. Relationships are about getting along and understanding each other. Think about this: do you judge your guy friends harshly when they act like an ass or say something stupid? No. You probably laugh at them. You might even argue a bit. But then you accept them for who they are and the things they do. That is what friends do.

You need to encompass all of those things and put them directly into your relationship with your partner. By accepting your partner as your friend you acknowledge her as an equal. You shouldn't expect her to change for you either. Overlook the little things—her quirks/idiosyncrasies—that bother you. Are they really that big of a deal? Then remind yourself of why you fell in love with her to begin with.

So the real secret is to take that same basic concept that you have with your friends and bring it into your relationship. By doing this, you'll **never** be called a bad apple.

True love really is very hard to find. No matter what you might think, the grass is almost never greener on the other side of the fence. If you think of your relationship as your yard, and you learn how to properly maintain it, your grass will be the greenest and most lush in the neighborhood.

No matter how great or average your relationship is, it can always use a little improvement. It takes time to enhance your relationship and make it stronger. This book will give you the details and steps you need to begin making it happen. Your awareness of each other's feelings will increase, which can only help both of you to grow as individuals within your relationship.

Open your heart and mind

I want you to rejuvenate your spirit through sensible, everyday methods and common sense. The bottom line is, you are not in a healthy relationship until you are friends with your partner. You may have to work at it, but it will pay off in the long run.

I will delve more into friendship as a foundation later in this book, but one thing you can begin doing right now, today, is talk to your partner. Tell her you want to be her friend, you want to listen, and you want her to listen to you. Even more importantly, show her that you are the man that's different from the rest, the man who will make her forget all her previous bad apples.

2 | Qualities of a Good Man

"Man is what he believes ..."

George Herbert Allen

A good man understands that a woman is not a possession, but a compliment, and most beautiful when permitted to be ALL that she can be.

Is a good man really that hard to find? If you ask nearly any single woman this question, you'll likely hear a resounding "Yes!" After all, as discussed in the prior chapter, nearly all women have more than one "bad apple" story to share, and every time a woman experiences a relationship with a bad apple, she has a tendency to become a little more jaded. Over time, the possibility of finding a good man seems about as remote as finding a needle in a haystack.

But, that doesn't necessarily mean that good men don't exist. They just may be a little harder to find primarily due to a lack of identity because of the environment we live in. Men are portrayed as dominating; sensitively is seen as a weakness. With so many conflicting messages in society about how men behave, it's difficult for them to define themselves with the values and qualities that they feel are important.

Notions of machismo, aggressiveness, philandering, and dishonesty constantly confront men in magazine articles, the movies and on television shows. It's amazing that any man can find a solid sense of identity, let alone focus on his good qualities. Taking a closer look at society, it's understandable that the messages men and women receive are muddled and confusing.

Men are typically portrayed as tough and rugged with big egos because in theory, the tough and rugged man is a hero. But how does that tough and rugged man fit into the normal, everyday household or in raising a family? He doesn't. At least, not in the way these men are depicted in movies and on TV. Typically, we're shown men arriving home from work, collapsing on their couches, drinking beers with their buddies while the women are running around taking care of the house and kids. In today's society, in addition to taking care of their children, most women have full-time jobs. But instead of relaxing they're taking on the full responsibility of maintaining their homes by themselves or with very little support.

When was the last time you saw a sitcom or drama that depicted a man sharing the household duties—helping out around the house, cooking dinner, taking care of the kids, or cleaning up? Chances are you can't think of one, and even if you can, you'll still see an uneven balance in the responsibilities between the man and the woman.

The real world is a very different place than the made-up world on our television screens, and while I'd like to think men are smart enough to see through these false representations, the truth is, it's more convenient for them to take the easy way out, even though they know right from wrong. Consider what effect this has on their relationships.

Every day we recalibrate our sense of identity as it relates to other people in order to adapt to what is going on around us and to fit in. This leads to the question: Is a man defined through competitive criteria set up by our culture to include his job title, physicality, car, or success? The answer is that these aspects provide an outward clue to his identity, so we use them to define him.

Many males today are confused by the mixed messages we get in relationships and in popular culture. Be strong, yet vulnerable; be the provider, yet share equality; take charge, but don't try to dominate.

The stereotypical modern American man might look something like a cross between John Wayne and football star Tom Brady. We are bred from the time we were young that the man has to be brave, strong, rugged, honest, tall and handsome—the stuff of legends or heroes are made out of. No wonder relationships go awry.

Your partner doesn't care if you drink a dozen beers while watching a football game. Therefore, it is critical that you are able to distinguish between your relationships, and what is valuable to the people you are with. In other words, think about your partner and what *her* values are when you're with her. Focus on bringing your good qualities to the surface. All men have good qualities, but often times they are hidden. Their qualities must have been there before. You did fall in love with them. So, where did they go? Why do people stop putting their best foot forward the longer they are in a relationship? Is it too much work to keep these qualities in the forefront in your everyday life?

Over time, we typically stop trying so hard with the one we're with. Relationships become complacent or lazy, from little things like the clothes we wear, our physical appearance, to things like listening and communicating. What happened to the things that made your relationship so exciting? How did you get into a rut and let all those good feelings fade into the background? Perhaps this is considered normal for most long-term relationships, but it doesn't have to be.

Be that Quality Man you and your partner deserve

So what are my secrets to staying in love?

- I stay grounded and thankful for the love she gives me.
- When I look at her I am reminded of how special she is and why I am in love with her.
- I think about all the good things we have done together.
- I realize how special my life is because she is part of it.

- Everyday, I appreciate that she is in my life and I let her know by telling her, and showing her love and kindness.
- I let her know by telling her, and showing her love and kindness.
- I try not bringing my ego or attitude into our home.
- I never forget how much I love and need her.

Think back to when your relationship first began. Were you friends then? Did you rely on each other for support, laughter and love? Do you still do so? Do you still find the time and effort to be there for them? If you answered "no" to any of these questions, where do you think she is going to go to fill these needs or voids? The answer is her friends, family or another man. Sooner or later she will replace you as her supporting role, most likely because you have not shown her the commitment and effort you once did. This is where relationships begin to break down, so this is where the initial work must begin.

You are not expected to be perfect all the time, but you must be willing to improve on each of the qualities that contribute to being a good man. By working toward these improvements, a healthier, happier relationship will result.

What does it mean to be a good man in the real world?

To answer that, let's answer some specific questions with help from your partner.

Grab a notebook or a sheet of paper and write your answers down together. It's important to visually see them in front of you, as that will help you later when we're discussing self-assessment.

- Name some qualities that describe a "good man".
- Name some non-physical qualities you most appreciate about your partner.
- What does your partner like about you? How is this similar to or different from what your friends appreciate about you?

Qualities of a Good Man

- What makes for a "great husband"?
- Name some qualities that you can ultimately work on to be a better partner.

The following list reflects what I consider to be important qualities necessary in a productive, healthy relationship:

- Communicating with consideration and empathy
- Active listening (fully paying attention)
- Respectfulness
- Self-confidence
- Good sense of humor and ability to laugh at yourself
- Positive outlook
- Honesty
- Loving
- Thoughtfulness (anticipating special occasions)
- Trust
- Interest in personal growth
- Patience
- Open-mindedness

The above is by no means meant to be a comprehensive list, as the combination of qualities you bring to your relationship will be unique unto you.

With your partner, go over the questions you previously answered and compare them with the above list of characteristics. Things to focus on in this discussion include:

- Which qualities do you and your partner excel at?
- Does your partner agree with your assessment? Do you agree with hers? If not, why?
- Talk about the differences and try to understand each other's point of view.

- Which qualities do you need to refine?
- Tell your partner what qualities you have that separate you from other men.
- Tell your partner which of her qualities separate her from other women.

This is a great time to discuss your relationship's qualities with your partner, and communicate your feelings, but be careful to keep everything under control. Have fun with it and keep anger out of the conversation. If things seem to be heating up, call for a break and come back to it later. This is meant to bring you and your partner closer, not increase the gap.

At the end, be sure to hug one another. You both deserve it.

Real Life Observations

Now that you and your partner have spent some time getting reacquainted and talking about the qualities you bring to your relationship, let's take a look at real life observations.

As you read the following scenarios, use them to reflect on your personal experiences. Maybe you will recognize yourself in these stories or maybe you have witnessed similar relationship scenarios. Try to visualize each incident, especially the negative elements of the interactions between these couples, so you can discuss them with your partner.

Keep in mind what you have learned about the qualities of a good man. What is your opinion on each scenario? What are the potential long-term negative effects on these relationships? Consider what is needed to strengthen their relationship with their partners and/or family.

Restaurant Scenarios

I was having dinner in a restaurant when I glanced around at the couples in the room. I was surprised how many of them barely looked at each other while they ate. In fact, very few of them behaved as if they even knew each other, much less liked each other. Very little conversation or laughter took place. I must admit, it was a disconcerting moment for me.

Scenario One

A couple that looked to be in their forties was sitting in the corner of the restaurant. I was able to see them clearly enough to recognize they wore similar wedding rings, and therefore, assumed they were married to each other. The woman was neatly dressed, and her faded, reddish-blond hair was pulled back to display pretty silver earrings. The man was wearing a deep blue, short-sleeved pullover with black twill pants, and his short, dark hair was sprinkled with threads of gray. As I observed the couple, it became apparent that the husband was not very interested in what his wife had to say. The wife, on the other hand, was smiling and looking at her husband, trying to engage him in conversation. But as she spoke, he made very little eye contact with her. Instead, he showed more interest in the food on his plate. She made several attempts to capture his attention before eventually giving up, simply staring off into space with a bewildered, sad expression on her face.

Scenario Two

On the other side of the restaurant, a young couple in their late twenties was having dinner with their two children. A beautiful blond-haired girl, maybe five years old, sat to the right of the mother and a little boy with brown, curly hair sat in a highchair to her left. Mom was busy trying to cut the food on the plates and feed the children. The man, who I assumed was the woman's husband and father of the children, sat staring at the television mounted on the wall, watching a baseball game. He barely seemed to notice the flurry of activity at his table. His wife's food sat untouched for at least fifteen minutes, probably growing cold, as she tended to the children. Eventually, she was able to eat a few bites, yet he never offered to help take care of the children to allow her a few uninterrupted minutes to eat.

Reflection

Take a few minutes with your partner to reflect on these two scenarios. Discuss each one, focusing on both the woman and the man in each situation. Share your opinions, as well as the scenario in general. Are there any the negative elements of the interactions described in each scenario? Did you feel empathy, if so, with whom?

Now, come up with a healthier response for each scenario. Have you been in a similar situation or treated a partner in a similar way? If so, just take notice of it for now, own up to it, and then, later we'll work on changing it. Remember, in order to become a better friend to your partner, you need to be aware of your actions and honest in your self-evaluations. This requires your willingness to work on turning your negative characteristics and habits into positive ones, as well as improving on each of your best qualities.

My Thoughts on These Scenarios

Granted, all I experienced was but a moment of these couples' lives. And while I have no way of knowing for sure if what I saw was the norm for them, it was painful for me to watch them.

While the men were physically present and taking up space, they chose to be mentally and emotionally detached from their partners and family members. To an onlooker, they showed that communication with their partners and children was not important to them. They showed little respect toward their partners in terms of listening and caring. They made no effort to show interest in the dynamics of their relationship or family. They ignored the one person who loved them the most.

I wondered how these couples could drift so far apart that they stopped communicating. There had to have been chemistry between them once upon a time. So how could a loving relationship change so dramatically?

The husband in the second scenario really bothered me. Why would he not want to help his partner care for his children? He seemed more interested in the baseball game. It didn't seem to matter to him that his wife could barely eat her own meal. My heart went out to the wife and children in empathy. I thought if that man continues to be unaware of his actions his marriage will someday be in trouble.

A Thread of Hope

Later that same evening, an older couple in their 70s, early 80s were getting ready to leave the restaurant as I was paying my bill. To my delight, the husband opened the restaurant door for his wife as they were leaving. As I followed them out to the parking lot, I noticed he held her hand all the way to their car. They walked slowly, while chatting and exchanging smiles. When they reached the car, he opened the door, helped her into her seat, fastened her seatbelt, and then carefully closed the door. I could not help but smile, seeing his obvious concern and consideration for her comfort and safety.

Now that is what love is all about

To me, *being a man,* in the best sense of the word, means achieving and utilizing all of the qualities that make a man *good* and using those qualities every day with everyone, especially in your personal relationship with your partner and family.

We've already discussed what many of those qualities are, but in this instance, I'm specifically speaking about communication. An open mind will help you learn to be a good listener and communicator. Sometimes it's tempting to interrupt your partner when she is trying to explain something, but you aren't truly listening if you are already thinking about your response before she's finished talking. Be patient, respectful, and loving as you listen, and try not to lose your sense of humor when you have a discussion. Trust me, guys; learning to listen to your partner will help you and your relationship more than anything else I can suggest.

There's one more scene I want to share with you. Just as before, visualize and think about your feelings about the scenario, then discuss with your partner how you would handle it.

The Forgotten Phone Call

This anecdote represents an example of how jumping to conclusions can lead to trouble in a relationship. When we give our partner the benefit of the doubt, we find that our patience and understanding pays off tremendously. This is also a lesson in friendship, good communication and respect, which are hallmark qualities of a good man and partner.

One day while I was on my way home from work, I called Susan on her cell phone just to say "Hi." She was in her car, so we chatted for a while. We were still talking when she arrived home. As she continued to chat with me, she struggled to hold the phone to her ear as she walked in the front door, her hands full with other belongings. After she'd let herself inside, she asked me to hold on for a second so she could greet her daughter and put down the things she still carried.

"I will be right back," she said.

Waiting on the other end, I heard all kinds of noise and commotion. So I waited and waited for what seemed to be ten minutes, chuckling to myself. I assumed Susan had forgotten about me in her flurry of arriving home. Deciding to call the house phone, I dialed the number and waited for her to answer.

"Hello," she said.

I laughed and asked her if she had forgotten me.

"Oh, my god," she laughed. "I started talking to my daughter and totally forgot about you."

I continued laughing.

"I am so sorry honey," she said in humor. "My daughter started telling me about her day and I got sidetracked."

We both continued laughing. Rather than get upset about something so meaningless, we found humor in it. I could have gotten angry, but because I didn't, we can still laugh about it to this day.

Maintaining a good sense of humor and a positive outlook on life is essential and, more than just a mind filled with positive thoughts, it's an attitude and a way of life.

Summary

If you picture yourself happy, you will become happy. Remind yourself of all the nice or cute little things you love about your partner. Remember why you fell in love with her in the first place. Consistently remembering your answer should put a smile on your face for a lifetime. Focus on the big picture. *Love* her in the best and most complete way you can.

> **Being born male does not make one a genuine man, unless he exemplifies the proper qualities of a good man.**

Traditionally, the man is the stronger member of the relationship. A man who accepts and enjoys the responsibility for a wife, a partner and children will find his role bringing great satisfaction. To achieve that satisfaction, you will need honesty, determination, generosity of spirit, capacity for compassion, knowledge of right and wrong, courage, wisdom, and gentleness. Sounds like a lot, but by taking it one step at a time, it can definitely be achieved.

Being the "good man" in a relationship or a family is no different than being the coach of a baseball team. Seriously guys, you show your coaching wisdom by being positive and constructive with your players. The same should hold true for your partner and family. Yelling at players, partners, or children is counter-productive. That same fulfillment a coach feels helping his team learn, grow and be supportive when they fail is an important and necessary ingredient in any relationship.

Remember, *a good man* will let all walk before him, "the children, the defenseless, and the underserved." He will demonstrate qualities of courage.

Courage ... the willingness ... to laugh ... to cry and open your heart to someone

If you can master the majority of qualities that are essential to a good relationship, you will become best friends with your partner. As you become more aware of how you interact with your partner and willing to open your mind to change, you will find a special friendship emerging that will thrill you both ... and that will bring you and your partner more happiness than I can quantify.

IF YOU NEED …

If you need conversation,
I will speak with you …
If you need a sounding board,
I will listen to you
If you need to laugh,
I will humor you
If you need to sleep,
I will relax you
If you need to dream,
I will fantasize with you
If you need to be alone,
I will provide space for you
If you need confidence,
I will support you
If you need to feel human touch,
I will hold you
If you need to feel passion,
I will excite you
If you need that Special Someone
To fulfill your needs
I am always here for You.

3 | Self-Assessment

"The greatest discovery of my generation is that man can alter his life simply by altering his attitude of mind."

James Truslow Adams

My hope is that by this point you're ready to dig in and get started on making some changes in yourself and in your relationship. But keep in mind it is not about your ego or pride. It is about being the best person you can be. Look at your partner and tell her that her love is worth it. If you consider your relationship to be strong at the moment, that's terrific, but that doesn't mean there isn't room for improvement. In fact, the day you or your partner decides that your relationship is "perfect" or neither of you no longer needs to try, will be the day your relationship begins to fail.

Do You Play Golf?

Do you try to improve your game by going to the driving range and putting greens? Why, to make your golf game better. You practice because you don't take your golf game for granted. Can you say the same thing about your relationship with your partner? How often do you practice improving your relationship with the one you love?

> **Is chasing that little white ball more important than the person sleeping next to you?**
> **Think about how much more fun it would be if you chased her around with the same intensity.**

We have all had past relationships that just weren't "right." If you are between relationships right now, this is a good time to assess your past relationships and your role in their demise. Take what you have learned and bring them into your next relationship. Have you ever asked yourself, what could I have done differently or better? To answer that question, and to begin the process of change, we first have to take a long and honest look at ourselves.

What Type of Man Are YOU?

We've looked at the qualities of a good man. Now, you need to take a serious look at yourself. It's critical to know where you've been before you can take any steps toward where you want to go. Remember, honesty is a key factor here, so we're going to go into this with a "no holds barred" attitude.

Change is all about attitude

To begin, write down an honest assessment of what you think you contribute to your current relationship. If you are not presently in a relationship, consider your last relationship and use that as your guide. Here are some ideas to get you started.

- What percentage of your contributions to your relationship would you rate as positive?
- What percentage of your contributions to your relationship would your partner rate as positive?
- What percentage of your contributions to your relationship would you rate as negative?
- What percentage of your contributions to your relationship would your partner rate as negative?

Real change begins with you. You cannot be in a great relationship unless you are a great partner, so for now, you're going to focus

Self-Assessment

on yourself, not your partner. Your partner's role in your relationship is important, but your primary objective at the moment is yourself.

By working on yourself, you'll greatly influence your partner to work on her own personal growth as well. You'll set a standard she'll want to follow. Then, after careful introspection and extensive consideration of who you are, you can begin to think about the traits and characteristics of your partner.

First, identify your traits—the good ones and those that need improvement. Before you can chisel away what needs improvement and strengthen the good, you need to know where you stand NOW.

Unfortunately, you can't look into a mirror and see your inner qualities as easily as you can view your outer physical characteristics. Therefore, identifying your personality traits will likely be one of the most difficult experiences you face throughout this process, but it can be done. If you've come this far, then that means you're serious about becoming the best person you can be for yourself as well as for your partner.

Assessing Your Personal Characteristic Traits

So you're about to honestly appraise yourself and your characteristics. Knowing where you want to end up is the easy part, but you can't get there until you know from where you're starting.

If someone calls you up and asks for directions to your house, you can't tell them if you don't know where they're coming from. Think of the process as a journey and that you're creating a map for yourself to get from here to there. Along the way, you're going to need a great deal of honesty, curiosity, strength, and humor in order to make it to the end.

On page 22, you'll find a *Personal Traits Chart*. This chart should be used to assess yourself. I've created a fairly complete listing of traits, but if I have missed some that you feel are important, feel free to add them in and rate them along with the rest. There are spaces for you to fill in other traits you feel are important. Rate yourself in each of the following categories on a scale from 1 to 5, with 1 needing the greatest improvement, and 5 meaning that particular trait is mastered or does not currently need attention. Be sure to circle whether you're willing to work on any of these traits or not.

Take your time and be honest, open, truthful, and critical. If you soften your answers, you'll only hurt yourself, your partner, and your relationship in the long run.

Chart A: Personal Traits

TRAIT	SELF-ASSESSMENT	WILL WORK ON?
Communication	1 2 3 4 5	YES NO
Listening	1 2 3 4 5	YES NO
Respect	1 2 3 4 5	YES NO
Self-Confidence	1 2 3 4 5	YES NO
Sense of Humor	1 2 3 4 5	YES NO
Positive Attitude/Outlook	1 2 3 4 5	YES NO
Honesty	1 2 3 4 5	YES NO
Trustworthy	1 2 3 4 5	YES NO
Compassion	1 2 3 4 5	YES NO
Thoughtfulness/Caring	1 2 3 4 5	YES NO
Desire for Growth	1 2 3 4 5	YES NO
Patience	1 2 3 4 5	YES NO
Open-Mindedness	1 2 3 4 5	YES NO
Word Choices	1 2 3 4 5	YES NO
	1 2 3 4 5	YES NO
	1 2 3 4 5	YES NO
	1 2 3 4 5	YES NO

The Results

After you've completed the above chart, take some time to look it over. Feel free to discuss your choices with your partner explain to her why you made those choices. Part of communication is having her understanding you more. Discuss the traits you feel you're lacking or need improving on.

Don't let the very thought of change worry or scare you. Change can be intensely terrifying, frustrating and difficult at times. One of the ways you can make change less scary is by working to maintain your sense of humor, a good mood, a great attitude, and positive thinking. Changing yourself is so much easier if you can smile and laugh at your shortcomings while you go about the process.

At this point, assuming you've filled the chart out with complete honesty, it's time to congratulate yourself. Few people are able to take this initial step, let alone move beyond it.

If, for example, you gave yourself a "1" or a "2" on the trait of "Listening," and you circled that you want to work on this, that's a good thing. Just because you have recognized you're not the best listener doesn't mean you are a bad person. Rather, you're a good person because you *have* recognized it and you're willing to make a change. Not only are you willing to be honest with yourself, but you're willing to forge ahead for the sake of enhancing your relationship.

All of the traits listed on *Chart A* are important. But there are some that are more essential than others. So, let's take a closer look at some of what I consider the more important aspects of this chart, as well as the pitfalls that can occur within each one:

Communication

Webster's Dictionary defines communications as: "The exchange of information between people, e.g. by means of speaking, writing, or using a common system of signs or behavior."

Developing a strong, open dialogue of communication with your partner based on the foundation of friendship is **critical**. If you currently don't consider your partner your *best friend*, then without friendship, true, positive communication cannot evolve between you and your partner.

Whereas most women have the art of communication within relationships fairly mastered, very few men are able to develop this trait or find it necessary. Women show more emotion and sensitivity. They love sharing their feelings. Most communication with their partner often revolves around feelings and sensitivity.

On the other hand, most men have a difficult time sharing what they really feel with the women in their lives. Again, this reflects on the "tough and rugged man" message men are raised with. Learning to communicate their feelings is something that every man needs to understand and work on.

It's likely you don't have any problems communicating with your buddies, right? You probably become embroiled in small talk with the guys on a regular basis. But when was the last time you sat down and had small talk with your partner about life or current events, let alone your feelings?

If you find talking to your partner unimportant, unnecessary, and/or difficult it doesn't have to be. Start off with easy topics and let yourself ease into the deeper discussion. I love talking to my partner. We lay in bed watching TV and talk during the commercials. We talk about all sorts of things—the program we are watching, about our day, or how nice it is just laying in bed together. We call it "*visiting*" and we do it all the time. Our friendship continually grows and stays alive and it brings us closer together emotionally.

If you have a friendship with your partner it won't be hard to find words of kindness and appreciation.

Careless Language

Careless language or choice words is a dangerous habit that can cause lifetime damage to a relationship. Words have the power for creating happiness or scars. If you are careless with your words, you will have a more difficult time discussing problems or issues. By choosing your words carefully with your partner in mind, you will demonstrate that you are sensitive to the conversation and to her.

As men we stick our foot in our mouth and before we know it, it's too late to take it out. Have you ever said anything unpleasant about one of her friends or a member of her family and regret it instantly? Have you called her names out of frustration? The first thing to do is realize you overstepped your boundaries and the best thing to do is to immediately apologize.

Self-Assessment

If you have made it a practice to treat your partner as a friend, she will be willing to believe you and accept your apology. Ask her to help you avoid the unfortunate practice of putting your foot in your mouth or as I would refer to it as the *"Male Hic-Up"*. Perhaps you can agree on a look or a gesture that she will give to let you know you are dangerously close to doing it again. She will feel positive that you are asking her to help you change the things YOU *want* to change, and she'll be more forgiving of your mistakes and encouraging of your growth.

Can you see how these little building blocks of knowledge or enlightenment can help you construct a solid foundation for a better relationship and a better you? As you continue in the right direction it gets easier. Not every man would care enough about his partner to take the time and effort to become a better friend.

I hope you're feeling emotionally charged right now and you are starting to see things differently. By going this far, you are already on the path of improving every aspect of your relationship.

Listening

Just as important as being able to communicate to your partner is the art of *listening* to your partner.

> **Webster's Dictionary defines *listening* as to concentrate on hearing somebody or something, or to pay attention to something and take it into account.**

Notice the words used in the definition, **"to concentrate or to pay attention."** Listening can be difficult. Most of us need to do a better job of it. Do you really concentrate on what your partner says? Do you pay attention as she tries to explain her opinion, needs, or wants? Let's be honest, most men could do with a crash course on listening to their partner from time to time.

How many men really listen to what their partner has to say and are willing to accept feedback? For whatever reason, men don't want to believe that a woman's opinion or her point of view is as important as his. If you don't believe me, think about your friends and their comments toward their partners' viewpoints or opinions.

Another problem is that men often do not allow their partner the time or the consideration to express her full view or opinion of the problem or issue. It seems we are born with having to control our environment. We have a tendency to interrupt women and try to get them to agree with us. We can only change this habit by paying attention and noticing when we do it, and the best bad habit killer is asking for help from your partner and not getting angry when she makes suggestions. By valuing her thoughts and opinions and giving them your total attention when she shares them, you will improve your relationship in ways you cannot imagine.

Solving Communication Problems

Most men like to solve problems. Whether it's why the right front fender is making a noise, or why the gas mileage per gallon has dropped, men like to feel in charge and in control. Your communication and listening problems are no different. You need to take charge if you want to solve your communication problems. Here's a quick tune-up list to get you started:

Develop the willingness to:

- discuss problems openly;
- take responsibility for your part in the creation of the problem;
- to take the necessary action to resolve the problems;
- pay attention and listen; and
- repeat back to her what you heard her say.

A man who listens:

- pays attention when his partner is talking;
- makes a sincere effort to consider her words for their meaning and intent;

- has the ability to listen to her opinion without trying to change her mind;
- acknowledges that he understands what she is saying, without arguing or trying to impose his viewpoint; and
- wants her to have her own thoughts, opinions, and ideas.

R-E-S-P-E-C-T

Along with communication and listening is a little word with a huge meaning: Respect. As the song goes, everyone needs respect. It's another building block towards building the necessary foundation to a great relationship.

When a man is respectful, he:

- is aware of both sides of any issue, never berating his partner for having a differing opinion;
- is always kind and considerate of his family, others, and especially his partner;
- is aware and supportive of the work his partner does around the house and how she takes care of the children;
- is respectful of her job, friends, and family;
- treats hers as an equal on all levels;
- realizes that respect has a way of intertwining into his everyday life; and understands that it is just as important to respect his partner as himself.

Respecting your partner should never be taken lightly. Respect has a way of branching out and affecting everything in your relationship, including attitudes and feelings and goes a long way toward solving problems.

> *What helps respect grow is to be open-minded.*

Being open-minded means you are:

- open to self-improvement;
- willing to look at issues from your partner's perspective;
- not too quick to judge; and
- not always having to be right and you partner is always wrong.

It's also essential to understand that you cannot be respectful of your partner and be controlling or dominating. Therefore, your EGO needs to go away forever.

A man who wants to control or dominate his partner will:

- tell his partner what she should wear;
- tell her how she should behave and what she should do and say;
- try to impose his will on her;
- try to control who she speaks to on the phone;
- try to control who comes over to visit and even pick their friends.

If you are in a relationship where you exhibit any of the above behaviors, you are hurting your partner, your family, and yourself. Many women will not tolerate this type of behavior. Why would anyone want to be in a controlling relationship where they were not treated as equals?

If you have a tendency to be dominating and controlling, you need to take a long look at yourself. I am sure you really don't want to be this type of person.

If you are opinionated you:

- believe you are always right;
- are unable to accept or see value in her opinion; and
- tend to be uncompromising and unable to look at situations from her perspective.

Self-Assessment

While your opinion IS important, so is hers. Therefore, you should listen to her side, just as she should listen to yours. Then, together, you can make a decision with all opinions being considered. This is called *compromise*, and it's the way all successful relationships function.

Historically, men have been the aggressors in trying to dominate the world. We've learned to be stubborn, generation after generation. We always want to be right. No one is always right, including you and me. But because of this socialized way of thinking, the lack of respect toward our mate has a trickle-down effect. When was the last time you sat down with your partner and openly discussed a problem or current issue between you, calmly and logically like you would with a business partner or buddy?

As we practice this change of attitude, we open ourselves to learning and this empowers your partner. When you can learn to communicate openly about your feelings, listen to your partner fully, and respect her for the amazing person she is you'll find not only your relationship blossoming, but you will become empowered to continue to change in very significant ways.

> **GROWTH is an amazing thing!**

Real-Life Outtake

Here's a personal anecdote to illustrate the lack of respect, poor communication, and a domineering attitude.

Susan and I were at a restaurant eating dinner one evening. She had chicken and I had seafood. It was one of the best meals I've ever had, and I wanted to offer her a taste of it. The following is the conversation that took place right after I tried to get her to try a bite of my meal:

"I don't like seafood, honey," she said.

"Have you ever tried it?" I asked.

"No. I don't even like the smell of it."

So what did I do? I pushed a little more. "Just one bite, you might like it."

"No, I don't want any."

"Well how do you know if you've never tried it," I asked, still pushing, like a jerk.

"What are you, my father? I don't like seafood. I never have," Susan said, giving me that look to just drop the conversation.

The mood of our romantic dinner changed and I realized I'd made a BIG mistake. I should have let it go when she said she didn't like seafood, but instead, I kept pushing her. In my defense, I just wanted to share something with her that I found delicious. But it was still wrong because I didn't bother to have all the facts. I was being pushy, controlling, and disrespectful, and, yes, I apologized. After that she was kind and smart enough to understand my *"male hic-up"* reasoning. We talked about it, the situation was straightened out, and our romantic evening came back to life.

As small as that may seem, it was a symptom of a bigger problem with me: that male dominating, controlling attitude. The old me wanted to force things on her for no apparent reason even though Susan was not crazy about seafood. After that incident, with her help and talking about it, I became more aware of my actions and the consequences they created. So I decided to make a conscious effort be more aware of my comments, and as a result, I have grown and become a better person and partner.

Recognizing Pitfalls

We all have pitfalls, and so do our relationships. Just like the story above, the important aspect is in recognizing these pitfalls and then taking the proper action to handle them. Going back to *Chart A*, if you found you scored low in a particular area, don't worry; it's okay. Being aware is what personal growth is all about. Instead of getting mad or being in denial, stop and think about why you scored low and ask your partner for some positive input. Awareness is the first step to change and we ALL have room for improvement.

Let's take a look at some of the common pitfalls outside of gaps in communication, listening, and respect.

Self-Assessment

Jealousy

One of the biggest problems in any relationship is jealousy. If you give in to it, jealousy will have a profound and long-term negative effect on your relationship.

> **Webster's Dictionary defines *jealousy* as an emotional state consisting of fear and anger, based on a subjective appraisal of a threat or loss of some aspect of a highly valued relationship with a partner to a rival.**

Consider These Hypothetical Scenarios

You are attending a social event with your partner when you notice another man smiling at her. Your partner returns the man's smile, which is likely nothing to stress over, as chances are she's simply reacting politely. Or you are out with her and another man engages in a conversion with her or maybe even try to pick her up. Now, ask yourself these questions:

- How would you handle this?
- Is your first reaction jealousy?
- Would you be mad at her or blame her?
- Do you love your partner enough to trust her?

How you react here is important. If, for example, your first reaction is to blame your partner for her appearance, or that she was flirting, that's a sign of jealousy, rather than trust. Jealousy can make you believe that somehow she enticed the other man to look at her and smile. If you think that's crazy, you're right. To me, it is a compliment if another man looks at my partner. And don't forget, she is going home with you, not him.

Ask yourself, why does this happen? Most often, the answer lies within our own feelings of insecurity. We all feel insecure from time to time. If I experience jealousy, I share it with Susan immediately. She always comforts me, gives me a kiss and reminds me how much she loves me and that I have nothing to worry about. By the time we are done talking, the jealousy is long gone.

Here is another example. Have you ever felt out of place but your partner seemed to fit in? Or have you ever felt threatened because she was (or you thought she was) having a better time than you? Some men have a hard time dealing with their partner's ability to enjoy herself apart from them. Instead, watch her enjoy herself. *She is just as entitled to have a good time as you are.* Let her shine in the limelight, and be proud and happy for her. You will benefit because you will have demonstrated how much you trust and care for her. And she'll appreciate you more for allowing her to be herself and have a good time.

Besides, the jealousy wheel turns in both directions. By showing your partner the proper way to react in these types of situations, you'll set the stage for when she becomes jealous of the woman who smiles at YOU.

So, remember, don't get caught up in this false sense of self-doubt, especially if alcohol is involved. When men feel threatened, regardless of whether the threat is perceived or actual, we panic and try to control the situation, usually followed by an argument. These actions will compromise any relationship and gradually weaken its foundation. Unless your partner has given you real reason for not trusting her, work on setting your feelings of jealousy aside.

> **Love is trusting her with your Heart and Soul.**

The Traditional (Destructive) Male Values

Another common pitfall in today's relationships rests in the traditional, yet destructive male values that many men still function under.

Believe it or not, old-fashioned concepts of what is acceptable treatment of women are still in practice in relationships today. These concepts are at times prejudiced and destructive, and after a time, they become negative habits that are difficult to break. We've discussed some of them already: lack of valuing and respecting a woman's opinions and feelings; trying to force her to agree with you; aggressiveness in word or deed.

Another common male value is that the house is "women's work," and men don't do women's work. Do you help her with household chores or with the children's needs? Working doesn't give you a free pass anymore and don't tell me you are tired or you do the yard work and don't have the time. If you love and appreciate her you will find the energy and the time.

Another example of an old male value is not having to call her when you are going to be late. What percentage of men or your friends do that? Think about how you want to be treated and treat her the same way. It's the Golden Rule and it's never gone out of fashion.

Summary

It is never too late to grow and develop helpful tools that will allow more productive communication with your partner and a deeper friendship in your relationship.

Remember to be kind and honest. Set your intention to be constructive and helpful when talking or communicating with your partner.

While this may seem simplistic and straightforward, it can be difficult to achieve this kind of deeper communication in stressful situations. Just remember to communicate with your partner and talk to her as your best friend. If you have to, slow down and even postpone some of the discussions to a less stressful time, and don't let your emotions get the best of you. If you feel you cannot talk about an issue without becoming angry and raising your voice, tell your partner. This is a valid part of communicating. Ask for time to calm down and then take a break.

We began by looking at the qualities of a good man and assessing ourselves. Just like the quote at the top of this chapter said: *"You can alter your life by altering your attitude."* We've got real progress to show for our efforts. Now let's keep going.

4 | Analyzing the Health of Your Relationship

"In the long run, men only hit what they aim at. Therefore, they better aim at something high."

Henry David Thoreau

We've spent some time on self-assessment, mostly focusing on your personal traits. Now, we're going to take that a step further and look at the overall health of your relationship. At the end of this chapter, you'll find *Chart B*, which will help you gauge certain traits and characteristics, so you can make a determination regarding your relationship's health. In addition, I'm going to talk more about communication and listening, because they are the cornerstones of building a strong friendship, which in turn is a necessary foundation to having a successful romantic, long-lasting relationship.

But first we're going to take a deeper look at some of the aspects that might be hurting your relationship, as well as give you some need-to-know basics so you can begin a path toward change. Going over these now will give you a better perspective for accurately filling in *Chart B*.

Identifying Problems Within Your Relationship

Identifying and confronting the problems within your relationship can be sensitive and difficult. Some common issues that negatively affect a relationship include:

- not coming home at the agreed upon time;
- not calling home when out longer than planned or expected;

- not participating in family activities;
- using the majority of leisure time for your own personal activities;
- not sitting at the dinner table with the family;
- not performing a fair share of the household or child rearing duties;
- not hugging or kissing your partner in the way she deserves.

Disrespectful habits include:

- leaving the toilet seat up at night or not lifting the toilet seat up when urinating (Would you want to sit in your own pee?);
- talking negatively about your partner in public or to friends;
- flirting or looking at other women while in the presence of your partner;
- not opening doors for her.

Men need to be aware of what their bad habits are in order to improve their relationships. Nothing positive can come out of being disrespectful and can only cause friction between partners. This difficulty is only made worse when a difference of opinion raises tempers or creates a conflict.

> **If things get too heated, don't be afraid to ask for a timeout to cool down! Your partner will appreciate the fact that you want to keep things on an even keel, rather than allowing them to get out of control!**

What do you do once a conflict exists? How do you solve it? Is it a battle of wills or a fight to the end to see who wins? Or is it a rational discussion, weighing both sides, keeping each other's opinions in mind?

Conflict occurs in every relationship. How you handle the conflict is more important than winning the fight. You must learn to think before you speak or react. Don't you do this at work when you are talking to your boss? Try training yourself and your mind to listen first and then talk calmly.

One thing that works for me is, before I speak or react to a conflict, I try to remember why I love them and visualize all the cute, good things about them. This really works and helps me keep my temper in check.

Anger never solves anything; it just deepens the wounds. Men usually have a habit of jumping to conclusions or automatically getting defensive about the topic of discussion. Do you yell a lot or bring up other non-related issues, like old arguments or past issues? If so, stop trying to confuse the conversation by redirecting it through criticism. Learn to be aware and responsible of what actions or reactions your words and actions produce. Remember, one push creates another shove. Before you know it, emotions are flying wild. You have to realize aggression is part of human nature. So try not to fall into those habits.

A True Man Will Learn to Control His Temper

Once you start learning to do this, you will definitely begin to feel better about yourself, your friends, and your family. It might even rub off at your workplace.

In order to bring clarity on this issue, we're going to start with some basic questions that might highlight some of your problem areas when dealing with a disagreement and/or conflict. If your partner is present discuss each topic with them, and as always, be completely honest while answering them.

1. **Are you able to discuss your problems and feelings *honestly and openly* with your partner?**

    If you can't, then ask yourself why not? And don't tell me that men don't have to. That is bull. Your partner deserves honest communication from the heart. Anything less is total disrespect for her, and at that point you should be sleeping on the couch.

Ignorance is NOT being a man. If you can't or won't express your feelings, how will she ever know what the truth is?

2. **Are you willing to take responsibility for your part when there is difficulty in your relationship?**

   Or do you assume it is her fault? When was the last time YOU admitted you were wrong and apologized to her? This is a key step for being able to compromise effectively.

3. **Is your idea of an open discussion yelling during a heated or controversial conversation?**

   People stop listening when being yelled at. Instead of an open dialog, they close down inside and they'll eventually stop responding altogether.

4. **Do you allow your partner to express her opinion?**

   If so, do you take personal interest in what she has to say even if you don't agree? Show her the respect she deserves by listening to what she has to say. You never know, she might change your mind.

Together, you should establish ground rules to make sure that you both play fair. Keep it as lighthearted as possible, even when the discussion is serious. This is not the time to crack jokes. Keep the tone one of love and trust. Do not enter any discussion with daggers drawn; otherwise it will defeat the purpose. Most importantly, play fair. Try smiling and don't play games. Work it out and move on.

If you are fighting often with your partner, you really need to figure out why. People who are unhappy with themselves tend to dump on the ones who love them.

When communicating about one another's issues and/or problems within your relationship, be aware if you have children in the house. *Don't* argue in front of them. Children know more than they let on, more than they would ever show you. So be aware of your surroundings. Arguing can affect their emotional wellbeing.

You need to listen to each other's perspectives and each partner should have equal time to voice their opinion. Talk to her about what bothers you and why it bothers you. Then give her the same opportunity. Help one another to come up with an alternative, positive solution, and move on to find a compromise.

The Fine Art of Compromise

> **Webster's Dictionary defines *compromise* as an agreed settlement of a dispute in which two or more sides agree to accept less than they originally wanted.**

Compromising is as simple as giving a little while you take a little. There has to be compromise in every relationship. The objective is to bring the problems or issues into the open and to be able to discuss them calmly, find a workable solution and plan of action *together*. There should not be any cheap shots or backstabbing, do not take any constructive criticism personally, and try to remain positive and to find a peaceful solution to both sides of the problem areas.

Let's go through some areas that cause issues to arise within relationships.

Listening: It Takes Two

"We have two ears and one mouth so that we can listen twice as much as we speak."

Author unknown

"It's only through listening that you learn, and you will gain much more than you can by talk."

Epictetus, Greek philosopher, AD 55

We talked about the importance of listening in the previous chapter. This time, we're going to look at the issue of "not listening" in a more comprehensive way. Please answer these questions truthfully:

- Have you ever rolled your eyes when your partner is telling you a story or trying to explain something to you?
- Do you look away from her as she talks to you?

- When she has something to say, do you only listen sometimes?
- Do you feel what she has to say is unimportant or nonessential?

These are examples of what not to do. You wouldn't treat your friends, your coworkers, or other people in your life that way, and you certainly shouldn't be treating your partner that way.

If you learn to really listen to your partner and try to understand what she is saying, where she is coming from and keep all doors of communication open, you can solve many problems.

Let's reverse the situation. You are talking during dinner with your partner and another couple, discussing an important current event. Suddenly, you notice the other couple is not paying attention to your opinion or what you have to say. How would that make you feel right then and there? Perhaps unappreciated and disrespected? This is the same feeling a woman experiences when their man doesn't take an interest in their conversation, or contradicts and disparages their point of view.

Gentlemen, this is all about your *awareness and growth as an individual person*. Personal growth doesn't take anything away from your manhood. It can only add to your résumé as a man, a person, and a provider. Trust me, there is nothing like the look your partner will give you when she realizes you care about what she has to say. It is one of the best feelings in the world.

This is such an easy problem to rectify. While you are listening to her talk to you, look into her eyes, allow yourself to get caught up in her emotions and her beauty. The reward is priceless.

Keeping a Scorecard: The Kiss of Death

Keeping score is a technique used to alter or change the outcome of an argument to your advantage by constantly bringing up past negative situations during a confrontation. It can also be a form of backstabbing or lashing out, even if you don't mean for it to be. Regardless, it creates more stress and unresolved solutions in your relationship and leads to a "He said-She said" type of tantrum, where heated emotions take over the conversation.

By keeping score in your relationship, you will start to lose the communication that is necessary to resolve problems, as well as the love and respect she has for you, thus triggering a downward spiral of negative emotions that can lead to a disconnected relationship. Your partner will begin to feel bitterness toward you rather than love and certainly not friendship, and this will only create a frustration for both of you.

Scorecards breed resentment and nothing positive can come from them. In fact, you should metaphorically throw all scorecards away and keep them where they belong—in the trash.

Ego

Ego is an expression of yourself, self-esteem or pride, which is indispensable if applied correctly and positively. Having too strong of an ego never accomplishes anything positive and will sooner or later get in the way of your relationship.

How is your ego these days? Is it constantly getting in the way or leading to arguments in your relationship? Does your nature consist of dominating, thinking you are always right or even thinking you are better than your partner?

When it comes down to a man's ego, all maturity, sensibility and understanding can be thrown out the window where it becomes a stubborn character trait that gets in the way of clear thinking and judgment. A good example of this is when a man gets into a fight, all judgment and rationality is lost.

I'm sure if you give it some thought, you can recall moments in your life when your ego got in the way. If so, would you consider it more of an insecurity problem and the need to dominate the relationship?

The key is to leave your ego at the front door of your house every day; don't bring it into your home. When it comes to your relationship, your ego will cloud your mind of rational thinking, shut down communication and create a false sense of security. *Surrender your ego and always keep it in check.*

Venting

Why is it that men are allowed to vent, but when a woman needs to vent it's called *nagging*?

If you ever sat with a group of married men, there will likely be some discussion about their partners venting (nagging) from time to time. Why do men get to vent, but when women do, they are considered a pain in the butt? Don't you think women are entitled to vent just like men?

Do you let your partner vent when she needs to or do you think to yourself, "Here we go again"? What she's really trying to say is: "I had a lousy day and I need to let it out." And what she *needs* is for you to listen, be supportive, give her a kind word and maybe a hug. Whatever you do, don't take it personally; stay strong and focused on her. By making validating and showing her your support, you are being a *MAN*, and that is part of your job in the relationship.

Venting doesn't have to be done in a mean or angry way. Never direct your anger directly towards your partner. Pay attention to when and how you're venting. Have a sense of humor.

> **Have you ever looked in the mirror while venting?**

After you're done venting, notice the mood you and your partner are in. Do you feel better? Isn't it nice to have your best friend there to listen to you and to love you as well?

Nagging

Do you nit-pick or constantly criticizing your partner about the little things in life or around the house? It is so easy to blame or take things out on someone else. We have all been there, including me. We've all done that. We start nagging because something else in our life is making us unhappy. For me, I try to be aware of my not-so-good days or moments, so as not to take it out on my partner. Unfortunately, it doesn't always work, but when it happens I always apologize to her.

If you find yourself having a bad day, I recommend that you try to turn a lousy day into a good day by starting the process before you get home. Call your partner ahead of time so as to pave the way. Then, when you get home and walk through the door, ask her for a big, long hug, and a kiss. There is nothing better than that. Talk about it if needed. The last thing you want to do is go into a shell and isolate yourself, setting yourself up for creating a negative pattern. Get out of the house, go out for dinner, play with your kids, or create a romantic evening. All of this will help you feel better and you will be ready for the next day.

Can you see a positive pattern developing here yet? Do you know what else will happen? You won't come home in a bad mood, turning the house upside down, just because *you* had a bad day.

Negative Attitude

Negative energy attracts negative energy. For some people, negativity in a relationship seems to be the norm and is readily accepted. If you're angry and upset about things a great deal of the time, you need to find out why. Do some soul searching. Talk to your partner and ask for her support.

Don't blame your partner for your problems. She's not responsible for the little stumbling blocks you encounter in life. That's just the way life is. There's no reason for you not to be happy when you're still breathing and sharing a life with the one you love. It may be just a matter of refocusing your negative attitude into a positive appreciation for her and your life together.

Focus on the things in your life to be positive about. This might require a daily approach, as it takes hard work and effort to change. But in the long run, you and everyone around you will be so much happier for it.

Jealousy

We talked about jealousy in the previous chapter, but there are other areas I want to focus on here. Jealousy is a normal feeling; we all feel it from time to time. If you trust your partner, you have nothing to worry about. Like any other negative emotion, it's how you handle it when it strikes.

Jealousy can cause insecurity, detachment and confusion in one's relationship. No one wants to admit that they are a jealous person, and some people are better at curbing their jealousy than others. But as much as we try to fight against it, sometime you just can't help but feel it. What's worse is that jealousy can often make you act out against your partner even if your partner is innocent and has no idea why you are angry.

Most men are subject to jealous feelings and are insecure by nature when it comes to feelings of the heart. These insecurities can cause very harmful and unsocial behaviors if they are not kept under control. Instead of allowing jealousy to rule you, take control by talking to your partner about your feelings. Let her know why you feel the way you do. If you approach the topic calmly with the issue being yours and not hers, you won't feel threatened, she won't feel defensive, and she will be willing to give you the reassurance you need.

If you believe and trust your partner; you can conquer jealousy and keep it under control.

Bar-Room Chatter

What do you say when speaking to your friends or strangers about your partner and your relationship? Are you positive and upbeat? Do you say nice things about her or do you make fun of her and complain about your relationship? Conversely, by telling people how lousy your relationship is or by talking down about your partner, you will look like the jerk that you are. And, trust me, it WILL get back to her, one way or another. What comes out of your mouth—positive or negative—is a reflection of you.

Take time to talk to your partner and get her views. After all, if you heard from a friend that SHE bad-mouthed you to HER friends, wouldn't it hurt? Man up and don't be part of this game.

If you have a good relationship and you tell people how much you care and how special she is, people will respect you. You will be

I Need My Space

Men love to use the expression "I need my space," when the truth is they want to distance themselves from their partner, be less involved in family activities or hang out with the boys.

If you need to hang out in bars with your buddies and don't like coming home after work, you might have some serious issues. For certain, one thing you don't have is friendship in your relationship. Now this isn't to say that a night out with the boys here and there isn't healthy and balanced. It's only when that takes precedence over your relationship or family that it becomes an issue.

Trust

> **Webster's Dictionary defines *trust* as the position of somebody who is expected by others to behave responsibly or honorably.**

Good relationships rely on trust. It is the most important bond in terms of building an intimate relationship between partners. It is the anchor that holds the relationship in place. If you agree to honor and respect this bond, your partner will trust you with her feelings and thoughts. Without trust, you cannot move forward and develop as a couple. If you dishonor her by lying, cheating or deceiving, you will have violated this trust and everything else that stands for love in a relationship.

Does your partner trust you? Do you give her reasons not to?

Faithfulness

On the heels of trust is faith. Do you have 100% faith in your partner? Do you think her feelings are mutual? Faithfulness means being consistently trustworthy and loyal to your partner, marriage and duty to your family. It is in *your* best interest to make sure she always feels safe, secure and loved.

Cheating

What would it be like at home the day your partner found out you were cheating on her? Can you picture that look on her face? Can you feel the hurt and pain that you planted in her heart?

What does cheating really solve? How would you feel if the situation were reversed? Could you just laugh it off, pick up the pieces and continue as though it hadn't happened? Should she do the same? Would you be able to sleep at night, if *you* were the victim? Would you ever be able to trust someone else in a future relationship? *How could you betray something as sacred as your partner's trust in you*?

Guys, the consequences and the long-term effect of what you do and say have lasting effects. Think about how much damage you could cause and how hard it would be to repair her feelings.

Don't give your partner any reasons not to trust you. Love her with all your heart and soul by communicating and sharing your feelings.

If you are considering cheating, you must not really be in love anymore. The honorable action to take is—first get out of the relationship before you do anything else. And be honest with your partner!

The object is to bring the problems or issues into the open to discuss them and to find workable solutions together.

Now it's time to move on to analyzing the health of your relationship. On the following page, you'll find *Chart B*. This chart is designed to help you find the weak areas within your relationship so you can make positive changes.

After you have completed *Chart B*, ask your partner to do the same and place her answers under the partner column. This is a no-holds barred exercise. You want your partner to answer honestly about how she perceives you, so don't hold any of her answers against her.

Rate yourself and then let your partner rate you in each of the following categories, (1) indicating the greatest need for improvement and (5) meaning the skill is mastered or does not need to be worked on.

Remember to smile through the process. Don't forget why you fell in love with each other and the purpose of this exercise. Leave your attitude and ego outside and don't get mad at the results. It will defeat the purpose and begin a rift that will only escalate within your relationship.

| Chart B: Assessment of Your Traits Within Your Relationship ||||
Trait	Self	Partner	Average
Communication			
Discussing your feelings and problems.	1 2 3 4 5	1 2 3 4 5	1 2 3 4 5
Explaining clearly your wants and desires.	1 2 3 4 5	1 2 3 4 5	1 2 3 4 5
Not raising your voice or yelling.	1 2 3 4 5	1 2 3 4 5	1 2 3 4 5
Repeating questions or statements (nagging).	1 2 3 4 5	1 2 3 4 5	1 2 3 4 5
Carefully choosing words that are constructive.	1 2 3 4 5	1 2 3 4 5	1 2 3 4 5
Positive reinforcement.	1 2 3 4 5	1 2 3 4 5	1 2 3 4 5
Listening			
Allowing your partner to express her opinion.	1 2 3 4 5	1 2 3 4 5	1 2 3 4 5
Taking interest in what your partner says.	1 2 3 4 5	1 2 3 4 5	1 2 3 4 5
Acknowledging that you understand what your partner says.	1 2 3 4 5	1 2 3 4 5	1 2 3 4 5
Open-Minded			
Nonjudgmental	1 2 3 4 5	1 2 3 4 5	1 2 3 4 5
Opinionated	1 2 3 4 5	1 2 3 4 5	1 2 3 4 5
Willing to look at issues from another person's perspectives.	1 2 3 4 5	1 2 3 4 5	1 2 3 4 5
Open to self-improvement.	1 2 3 4 5	1 2 3 4 5	1 2 3 4 5

Trait	Self	Partner	Average
Problem Resolution			
Willing to discuss problems openly.	1 2 3 4 5	1 2 3 4 5	1 2 3 4 5
Taking responsibility for your part of the issue.	1 2 3 4 5	1 2 3 4 5	1 2 3 4 5
Willing to take action to resolve problems.	1 2 3 4 5	1 2 3 4 5	1 2 3 4 5
Maintaining the resolution.	1 2 3 4 5	1 2 3 4 5	1 2 3 4 5
Confidence			
Jealousy	1 2 3 4 5	1 2 3 4 5	1 2 3 4 5
Trust in your partner.	1 2 3 4 5	1 2 3 4 5	1 2 3 4 5
Attitude			
Controlling and/or dominating	1 2 3 4 5	1 2 3 4 5	1 2 3 4 5
Ego	1 2 3 4 5	1 2 3 4 5	1 2 3 4 5
Stubbornness	1 2 3 4 5	1 2 3 4 5	1 2 3 4 5
Honesty	1 2 3 4 5	1 2 3 4 5	1 2 3 4 5
Positive behavior	1 2 3 4 5	1 2 3 4 5	1 2 3 4 5
Thoughtfulness	1 2 3 4 5	1 2 3 4 5	1 2 3 4 5
Caring	1 2 3 4 5	1 2 3 4 5	1 2 3 4 5
Affectionate	1 2 3 4 5	1 2 3 4 5	1 2 3 4 5
Courtesy (Opening doors, etc.)	1 2 3 4 5	1 2 3 4 5	1 2 3 4 5
Patient	1 2 3 4 5	1 2 3 4 5	1 2 3 4 5
Attentive	1 2 3 4 5	1 2 3 4 5	1 2 3 4 5

Trait	Self	Partner	Average
Sharing Household Duties			
Laundry	1 2 3 4 5	1 2 3 4 5	1 2 3 4 5
Cleaning	1 2 3 4 5	1 2 3 4 5	1 2 3 4 5
Dishes	1 2 3 4 5	1 2 3 4 5	1 2 3 4 5
Grocery shopping	1 2 3 4 5	1 2 3 4 5	1 2 3 4 5
Helping with the kids	1 2 3 4 5	1 2 3 4 5	1 2 3 4 5

Analyzing the Health of Your Relationship

Trait	Self	Partner	Average
Respect			
Criticizing	1 2 3 4 5	1 2 3 4 5	1 2 3 4 5
Respect partner's feelings.	1 2 3 4 5	1 2 3 4 5	1 2 3 4 5
Respect partner's opinions.	1 2 3 4 5	1 2 3 4 5	1 2 3 4 5
Appearance			
Hygiene	1 2 3 4 5	1 2 3 4 5	1 2 3 4 5
Fitness	1 2 3 4 5	1 2 3 4 5	1 2 3 4 5

Now that you have completed *Chart B* with your partner, it's time to compare your answers. This might feel a little awkward or difficult, but it's an essential step that shouldn't be skipped. Remember, it is critical to know how your partner perceives you. Then, average your score with your partner's into one number in the last column. For example, if you have a "3" in one area, and your partner gave you a "1" on the same trait, then the average score would be a "2." Do this for every trait and every score.

Now, it's time to move on to the discussion portion. Talk over your scores with your partner. Discuss how you can improve the traits that you have scored low on. Together, choose which categories you need to work on first and give examples of how you can improve those categories you have agreed on. Then come up with a working timetable and solution, and ways to begin the process.

Don't be too hard on yourself. Be proud that you have come this far. No one is perfect and we all do or say dumb things from time to time. See the humor. Include in your discussion a memory of something that, in hindsight, now seems so ridiculous it's laughable. When you can laugh at yourself, you'll know you are making valuable progress.

Summary

Building and keeping a good, lasting, successful relationship takes work, understanding, compromise, flexibility, forgiveness, and most importantly, good communication skills.

Be a proud part of this solution.

You've already come a long way. By now, you and your partner should have opened up tremendously. Remind one another of all the good times you've shared together. Enjoy the process of making your relationship more fulfilling and happy. Celebrate your accomplishments and be proud of them.

5 | Friendship—The Foundation of a Healthy Relationship

"The only way to have a friend is to be one."

Ralph Waldo Emerson

All enduring relationships have one component in common: friendship. Not only is it the most important brick in building a strong foundation to weather out the storms, but it will create the nurturing environment that will help your relationship thrive, day in and day out.

> **Webster's Dictionary defines a *friend* as one attached to another by respect or affection.**

Real friends are there for you in good times and in bad. They rejoice with you when you have accomplishments and they help you stay level-headed when things go wrong or life becomes tough. Friends will haul boxes for you when it's time to move; they'll listen to you complain about your boss at work; they will remember and buy you a drink to celebrate your birthday. Most important, friends don't judge you. They accept you for who you are.

Through it all, they listen, share advice, and enjoy spending time with you. At the end of the day, they have your best interests at heart, and if you're a real friend, you feel the same way about them.

Can you see why it is so essential that your partner be your best friend and you theirs. There is nothing more critical to the growth and quality of a relationship than friendship.

Having a friendship with one's partner seems to be the exception in today's world. It is my intention to give you additional ideas to help you grow and strengthen this foundation in your relationship. Some are simple and basic with common sense; others are what have worked in my personal relationship. All in all, the idea of creating a fun and nurturing friendship with your partner should excite you.

So how do you go about building a friendship with your partner? Well, to have a friend, you need to be a friend. Learning how to be a friend and taking the steps to create this bond with your partner will take time and patience. It is far easier said than done, but the result will definitely be worth it.

While this chapter focuses on what you can do, friendships aren't one-sided. Your partner needs to be as equally involved in the process. If both of you work at being each other's best friend, you'll begin building the strong, stable foundation your relationship needs to truly flourish.

The Components of Being a Friend

We all have friends, right? Even if we're not overly social, there is at least one person we can count on as a friend. Some of us have a lot of friends, others of us have just one or two; but what's important here is quality, not quantity. Real friends aren't just there for the good stuff, but for the challenging times and all the moments in between. These are the friends that we want, and therefore, this is the type of friend you want to aim toward being.

For the most part, women instinctively have better interpersonal skills and tend to make lasting friendships easier than men. It's simply in their makeup to bond with other people. Men, on the other hand, tend to have a fairly large group of casual friends and only one or two they consider to be a true "buddy."

Friendship—The Foundation of a Healthy Relationship

If you're a guy reading this book, stop and think for a minute about the guys you've been friends with the longest—the buddies in your life. Believe it or not, all good relationships have the same base components, and it is those components I want you to identify. *Whatever it is that binds you to your buddies is the same sort of glue you need to create a friendship with your partner.*

Now I'm not telling you to create the same friendship with your partner that you have with your buddies, nor am I asking to treat your partner like your male friends. But the trust, respect, and affection that you have for your buddies are the same elements that need to exist in the relationship with your partner.

Let's take a closer look at the three main components that make up a friendship, so you can begin applying them to your relationship.

Communication

Communication is very important for building a healthy, loving and romantic relationship. Always talk things out between you and your partner no matter what the subject matter. This will help identify what areas need improvement in your relationship. Lack of communication will lead to misunderstandings and distrust.

You need to keep an open dialogue between you and your partner. Learn to talk to each other as friends do. This also includes feelings of the heart and listening. Communication can make or break any relationship.

> **Communication is the bridge that connects two people.**

The term "relationship" literally means shared connection. The best relationships work because they stay connected by communicating with one another.

Honesty

Always start and finish with telling the truth. Relationships that last are not based on lies, half-spoken truths, or embellishments. Honesty creates trust and respect between you. In doing so, here are some pointers about honesty to keep in mind:

- There are no half-truths she won't sniff out. If you're purposely leaving something unsaid, she'll sense it and she'll ask about it. If you continue to leave it unsaid, it will cause doubt, mistrust and tension.
- Being honest does not give you permission to be cruel. Be honest, but do so with compassion.
- If your opinion on something or someone is not favorable, take the time to explain why you feel the way you do. Even unpleasant truths are easier to handle if they can be understood.

If you and your partner can be honest with each other, trust will follow.

Trust
Trust isn't given freely; it's earned over the course of a relationship. As slow as trust is to build, it's often quickly destroyed with dishonesty, mental games, and cheating. If friendship is thought of as the foundation of a healthy relationship, then trust should be considered as the walls that hold a relationship together. Without trust everything else will fall apart and decay. *Without TRUST everything else will fall apart and decay.* Some people trust fairly easily, while for others it takes longer. Trust is based on a person's prior experiences. If your partner has been in several relationships where she was cheated on, getting her to trust you will likely take longer than it would with a woman who'd never had this experience.

Trust is a very tough element to control and to believe in for some people, especially men, and is tied to a myriad of emotions. Therefore, don't anticipate or assign trust, or the lack of it, before you truly get to know your partner. Doing so could create mistrust where there shouldn't be and can irrefutably harm your relationship.

Both of you need to work hard to clean the slate of past experiences and focus on your current relationship. This isn't easy but with perseverance, it can be done as long as you and your partner are consistently truthful, dependable, faithful and compassionate with one another.

The Daily Routine: Strengthening Your Friendship

You might think that with honesty and trust well in hand your friendship with your partner will grow easily. While honesty and trust are necessary, there are four additional elements that when practiced will create the best friend bond you and your partner should have with each other that take your friendship to that next all-important level.

1. **Embrace Growth.** You and your partner are in this together for the long haul. Therefore, be one another's advocate to challenge each other to grow spiritually, intellectually, and physically. Helping each other creates the balance in life that will make you happy and healthy people and will give your relationship amazing vitality.
2. **Affirmation.** Affirm each other's value. It's up to you to let her know how important she is, and it's up to her to let you know the same. Think of this as being her cheerleader by reminding her of how valuable she is to you. A simple "I Love You", will make her day.
3. **Respect.** Show respect for each other's feelings, wishes, and wants. You are her sounding board, and she is yours. When two people are able to show respect toward each other, especially in the face of disagreement, their relationship will grow by leaps and bounds.
4. **Encouragement.** Encourage each other through the use of compliments, good deeds, and honest, respectful behavior.

If you can be honest and trustworthy with your partner by affirming, encouraging and showing respect on a daily basis, you'll find your friendship will reach that next level where you will become one another's best friend.

Defining Couples and Boundaries

Your relationship with your partner is far different than what you share with your other friends, even with the foundation of friendship in place. But, what does that mean in terms of your relationship that you don't necessarily think about with your buddies?

> **Webster's Dictionary defines a *couple* as a pair of things or persons, from which in terms of a relationship means.**

I love this definition because it strikes the chord of exactly what a couple is. How often do we refer to our significant other as our "other half"?

It is nearly impossible to build a healthy relationship if either partner does not recognize that the other is worthy of equivalent value. Respect comes hand in hand with understanding and protecting boundaries. I'm confused as to why so many men have such a difficult time respecting their partners to the point where this disrespect often leads to compromising boundaries within the relationship of a couple.

As children we learned about boundaries from parents and teachers. Don't cross the street by yourself or don't ride your bike in the street. As we grew older, we begin to set boundaries for those around us. However, adults often forget the necessity and importance of boundaries in their daily lives. Without proper boundaries, we often struggle to maintain healthy relationships both personally and professionally. Boundaries are essential to our ability to properly manage our lives and make room for the things we desire.

Just as you want and need your own space and a bit of privacy, so does your partner. Many men seem to have a hard time with this issue, perhaps because of personal insecurities, or because of control issues. Regardless, boundaries are important and it is important to have them.

Friendship—The Foundation of a Healthy Relationship

Here are some tips about boundaries for the couple's relationship:

- Each of you should have the amount of privacy you're comfortable with. If she doesn't want to share what she and a girlfriend talked about, that's okay.
- Allow her to spend time with her friends and family. Don't feel threatened by her girlfriends. Be happy when she returns home and let her know that you missed her.
- Be flexible. Maybe she prefers to come home from work and have some solitude for a while. Every now and then, she wants some time on the weekend. In return, she should do the same for you.
- Don't take it personally. Some situations where you need to remember to allow her space include when she is in the bathroom, when she is talking on the phone, when her family visits, and when she is attending to a girlfriend who may be upset and needs her support.
- Just because your partner wants privacy in some of these areas does not mean she doesn't want to be with you.
- Just as you are the sum of your upbringing, so is she. Your family might be open but hers might not be. Learn who she is and work to understand the nuances that will make her the most comfortable.

Remember, boundaries are not there to alienate loved ones; they are an ally in keeping you healthy and happy as you engage with those who can enrich your life. Eventually, as the trust between you and your partner increases, your individual needs for privacy may dwindle or alter. The most important thing to remember is to respect one another.

Making Your Partner Feel Important

Do you let your partner know you really care on a daily basis? Out of common courteous this is mandatory and should be done consistently everyday, per conversation. All it takes is a kind word or gesture—buying flowers on her birthday or getting her an anniversary gift. The defining moments are the little things you do in a relationship that shows how much you care. You are thinking of them, and that is a sign of respect.

If you love someone, then you'll want her to feel good about herself, and you'll want to be the main person in her life who helps her feel that way. Everyone is happier when they're feeling positive and upbeat.

Here are a few ideas that will help you make your partner feel important:

- *Praising your partner* for what she does, when she does it. If she does something nice for someone, be aware, give her recognition and *compliment her.*
- Show her appreciation. Let her know how much you appreciate having her in your life, and tell her why. Call her and **leave a message** saying, "Just thinking of you and wanted to say hi." You don't need a special occasion to show your love, appreciation, or affection.
- Keep communicating. This includes listening. When you first met you talked all the time on the phone, through e-mail, on dates, etc. You listened tentatively to her stories. So why and when did you stop communicating? Start talking again. Share your thoughts and your dreams. Ask her about her day, her opinion on a movie or TV show you watched together, what she wants to do over the weekend, etc. If she's upset, find out why. Let her know you care by being there and being willing to listen.
- Surprise her with a token of your affection. It doesn't have to be expensive. It can be as simple as a card with a handwritten note or as elaborate as a weekend away in a fantastic bed & breakfast. **Flirt** with her. Every woman wants to feel sexy. Kiss her passionately at a time you normally wouldn't. She's sure to feel swept away and important.

Friendship—The Foundation of a Healthy Relationship

- Be supportive to what is important to her. You don't have to agree to everything, but support her.
- Be present in your relationship. Pay attention to her mood, her wants, and be the person she turns to with good or bad news. Show her you're there for her, no matter what.

By letting your partner know that she is important to you on a daily basis, you're solidifying the reason why you are together.

Summary

Once you become friends in your relationship, it will lead to feelings of increased mutual respect and equality. Gradually, you will both learn to be less judgmental and make allowances for each other, while becoming more patient and kind, embracing one another's smiles, laughter, and silliness. Having more understanding about whom she is will enhance the closeness of friendship and in turn heighten your love for her. You will stay connected longer because you'll enjoy each other's company more.

It is very important to remember that friends ...

- Are *always* supportive of each other.
- Always find a way to make it work, no matter how difficult the problem between them might be.
- Communicate and use each other as sounding boards.
- Respect each other.
- Don't judge one another.
- Find time to let each other know their value and importance.

By being your partner's friend it will unlock the doors of happiness and pleasure beyond your wildest imagination, not to mention enhance your romance. You will each become more supportive and helpful in nurturing your relationship and a beautiful rose will blossom.

6 | Make a Plan to Improve Yourself

"There is only one corner of the universe you can be certain of improving, and that's your own self."

Aldous Huxley

Now that you have a better understanding of who you are and what characteristics or traits you want to change, you are ready to put a plan together.

The following are questions you need to address with your partner. Her answers will help you set your plan for improvement and part of that means learning to compromise within your relationship.

Are You Ready to Change?

Before you can begin the process of change, you have to be aware of where you are currently and what you need to work on. Change is a process of baby sets.

Chapter Three, Self-Assessment, has helped you see where you are now and where you need to improve on. Set your goals high and have an end-goal in mind.

> Change can be scary, unsettling, and sometimes the process might seem too difficult to deal with. But by forging ahead, you'll find every portion of your life reaps the rewards, including your relationship.

Are you the type of person who is willing to share your heart, your mind, and your soul with your partner?

Consider these questions:

- Does your partner know you will always be there for her?
- Do you openly communicate and share your feelings with her?
- Do you support her emotionally and mentally?
- Are you willing to do what it takes to be a better man for your family and relationship?

What Type of Person Do You Want to Become?

Take a few minutes to look deep into your heart and ask yourself this question—and be 100 percent honest—Which characteristics would you like to improve on?

We all could fine-tune ourselves in some form or fashion. Don't be afraid to admit you need improvement. It is up to you to figure out with the help of your partner what you are willing to work on.

In general, women are more receptive than men when it comes to making changes. They are true to their feelings and are not afraid to express and share them. Women want friendship, laughter and conversation in their relationships. They do not size each other up or try to dominate the conversation. This is something we as men can learn from them.

Always remember how blessed you are to have someone who loves and cherishes you. Don't be a fool and mess that up. Don't take your partner, your relationship or your family for granted.

Gentleman of the House
The Ideal Man:

- must have strength of character as well as emotional strength;
- must have an honorable and respectful manner towards others;

- stands up for those he cares for and those who are in need of his help;
- must be gentle in nature, patient, slow to anger, loving, and kind-hearted;
- believes in communicating and listening to his partner;
- is fun-loving, adventurous, romantic and has a good sense of humor;
- supports her in her pursuit of her interests, even if he doesn't have an interest;
- shares his day-to-day experiences of work;
- will be supportive and positive through the speed bumps and challenges; and, most importantly
- he will be her best friend.

> *A gentleman is a civilized man who behaves with courtesy and thoughtfulness on a continual basis.*

A True Gentleman
Are these values part of your everyday behavior?

- Do you open doors for your partner on a regular basis?
- Are you respectful, kind and gentle toward your partner and the other people around you?
- Are you a role model to your children?
- Do you lead by example?
- Does your family look to you for kindness, wisdom, and positive leadership?
- Do you stay level-headed for the most part, being proactive instead of overreacting to situations?
- Does your family respect or fear you?

A true gentleman:

- understands and accepts his partner for who she is;
- respects her need of privacy and her own space;
- allocates her own identity and independence;
- is patient and nurturing when dealing with her emotions;
- doesn't put his partner down or talk negatively about her in public, in front of family or friends; and
- shows positive reinforcement to her self-esteem.

Open Discussion: What type of person do you want to be?

Compare your results from *Charts A and B*. This is an essential element for moving forward, committing to change, and creating your action plan for success together as a couple.

When sharing your results, be sure to do so in a friendly and cordial manner, discussing the positive and negative conclusions. Do not argue with your partner about her opinion or answers. Let her speak her mind. This exercise is not about defending yourself; it's about learning to grow as an individual through self-awareness. You, in turn, will have the opportunity to share your results with her as well.

> *Remember ... She loves you, and would not be working to improve your relationship if she didn't.*

As we've already discussed, the hardest part of change is admitting we need improvement. It's not a failure to admit so, but rather a healthy, positive step in creating the future you desire.

The second-most difficult part is identifying the attributes that you need to improve upon. Once that's done, and you've accepted them, the process can begin.

In most cases, both you and your partner will have more positive attributes than negative. Therefore, go ahead and focus on the positive first. This will create an environment of trust and communication, and will make the rest of the conversation easier to handle for both of you.

Be sure to reflect on the things you love about each other and why those things are important to you. The input you both share in this discussion will allow you a greater awareness of how you impact each other. In addition, if you both know your strengths as individuals then you will have a good sense of who should lead a particular portion of the discussion. In a greater sense, this awareness will allow your partnership to benefit emotionally, physically, and financially.

Negative Patterns

You cannot grow or change as a person if you're not aware nor willing to change the negative traits.

After you have discussed one another's positive traits, it's now time to work on the negative patterns of behavior. An example of a negative trait could be an attitude or a response to a given situation. If you keep doing the same things, or reacting in the same adverse manner, you'll continually achieve the same negative results.

I cannot stress enough that you need to be aware of the negative contributions that you inject into your relationship, which is why this discussion with your partner is so crucial. We all know it is difficult to hear anything negative coming from someone you care about, but try to keep an open mind and heart, and listen. Chances are even if you don't agree with your partner's assessment, you should be able to see why she feels the way she does.

Change negative behaviors by replacing negative words or attitude with a positive approach. Ask your partner to point them out when it happens. After a while you will be able to recognize them on your own.

Another important step is being able to admit when you are wrong. This will lead to an open dialogue between you and your partner. As I've said many times in this book, strong communication skills are essential to any healthy relationship.

Once you have an understanding of your negative traits, and are willing and able to admit to wrongdoings, it's time to look at some basics in your day-to-day life.

Day-to-Day Actions Make a Difference

Day-to-day actions will begin to change immediately while you're working toward your larger goal. Your actions—the attitude you bring into your home—will set the tempo for the entire day.

Smile, Reflect, Appreciate, Hug and Kiss

Ask yourself these questions:

1. How do you greet your partner when you first wake up in the morning?
2. Do you start the day with a negative comment, an argument, or a grouchy attitude?
3. How do you greet each other when you first come together after a long day apart? Even if the morning started off great, a lot of events happen in our everyday lives that can change the positive tempo of the morning. We all have bad days at work. Do you come home grouchy and irritable toward her because *you* had a bad day?

By readjusting your priorities and energy, your attitude will make a difference in your relationship and will have a positive effect. So, how do you make it a good morning or good evening every day? Here are a few pointers that have worked for me:

- If you live together, stop and visit with her first thing in the morning. You both may have hectic days ahead of you; five or ten minutes can really bring a happy light to start both of your days. Lay in bed for those extra few minutes and talk. Exchange kisses and hugs before heading out. If you're on different schedules, wake up when she does, even if only for a few minutes, so as to visit with her briefly and let her know you still care.

Make a Plan to Improve Yourself

- After your long days, even if you've had a rotten eight hours at work, greet her in a positive, loving manner before you get into a discussion about all the things that happened at work or are going on in the house. The first and easiest thing to do is remember that you love each other, and remember all the good feelings that come from her loving you, and you loving her. Talk about something good or funny that you shared together during the week. Before you realize it, your bad day will have turned into a pleasant evening.

> **We turn to our friends when we are having a bad day. Wouldn't it be nice to have a best friend at home?**

When you give your partner physical affection, you're impacting the mood in your home in the best possible way. You're telling her that you're glad to see her, that you're happy to be home, and that she is the best part of your day.

When you think about it, aren't you the happiest in your home? Isn't your home always a better place than work? If not, then you need to focus your energy on changing the atmosphere of your home immediately.

By implementing these positive, affectionate actions each day in your home, you'll begin to see the difference in creating a happy home for a lifetime.

Defining Your Goals

Now that you and your partner have openly discussed your situation, you should have a good idea of what your goals are. This section will require you to refer to *Charts A and B*.

There are two types of goals: *short term*, which are quick or easily changed or obtained; and *long term*, which take time and require some adjusting on your part.

Be patient with yourself as you begin to implement these changes. You've just learned these new skills, and the only way to master them is by practice, so don't be hard on yourself. As you become more comfortable with change and you start growing as an individual, the results will become visible in your relationship.

With the help of your partner, take into consideration the following questions for each goal you are aiming toward. Be as specific as possible as this will increase your chances of success from the onset.

1. What do you want to achieve and what results do you want?
   Be specific. If, for example, your goal is to have fewer arguments with your partner, state what you tend to argue about—money, going out, wanting more affection, etc.
2. Who, beside you and your partner is involved in the goal? Some goals might include other family members, friends, or coworkers.
3. When do you want to see the goal realized?
4. State your goal in positive terms.
5. What are the logical and chronological steps you'll need to take in order to achieve this goal?
6. Why are you setting this goal?
7. What stops you from having this goal right now?
8. How will you handle potential obstacles?
9. What is the method you will utilize to reach these goals? When you measure progress, you have a better chance at staying the course and reaching that finish line.
10. Do you and your partner have agreement on achieving these goals?
    When you and your partner are in agreement, it makes you accountable. Without accountability in place, chances are you won't see the goal through to completion. Therefore, every goal you set should be an agreed goal between you and your partner.
11. With every goal you choose to set, ask yourself if it is realistic. It can be a difficult goal, but be sure you have the ability, methods, and resources available to make it happen.

12. Is this the appropriate time in your life to work on this specific goal? Choose a timeline that you and your partner are comfortable with.

By incorporating the goals you and your partner have set you'll have definable, measurable goals that can be achieved. It's worth the time to go through these lists for each and every goal you choose to make.

Remember, while some goals might feel impossible, they're likely not. Don't let discouraging thoughts and attitudes get in your way of the future you want. By setting goals in a clear and concise method, you are paving your path toward success.

When you take the time to firmly and properly set a goal, visualize and feel it coming to fruition. Once this happens, your desire to succeed becomes even stronger.

A Plan for Action

Now that you have set some goals and are aware of your individual positive and negative characteristics, you and your partner can make a plan to build on the strengths.

1. As a couple, choose two or three negative attributes that you both believe would benefit your relationship if made positive.
2. Focus on the obtainable and the agreeable, and for now, let the other issues sit for later discussion.
3. Discuss these attributes and decide how critical they are to your relationship, then discuss possible solutions with your partner. If you need to, rate their urgency. Is there a weakness that is currently getting in the way of your happy home? If so, perhaps you might put this at the top of your list.

This process will help open the lines of communication, and will also improve your friendship.

This is a *Team Effort*

Do this using the following critical elements to begin with your first three goals in mind:

1. Break them down into achievable steps.
2. Take each goal one day at a time, one step at a time.
3. Decide on a day/time of the week to discuss how things are going.
4. Decide if any alterations need to be made.
5. Set new timelines if need be if you haven't obtained the outcome you desire.

As each goal becomes realized, choose the next most critical element on the list and repeat the cycle.

As you work through your goals, use the following methods to help you achieve success:

- Listening: A true gentleman listens and cares about what his partner has to say throughout the entire process. If you allow her to express herself honestly without creating negativity, she'll have more positive feedback for you. Listening allows you to be an active part of the solution, and together, you will find a workable method that will enable you to obtain your goals.
- Laughter: Laughter and humor is one of the keys to self-improvement. We all do silly things from time to time. These open-minded exercises, the goal setting and achieving process, will rekindle a new friendship and stronger relationship between you and your partner.
- Love: Remember you're doing this as a team because you love each other. You want to create a strong, nurturing relationship that will flourish. Hang onto that thought when the going gets tough.

If working on three goals at a time is too stressful, pick the most critical issue and focus on just that one for as long as need be. This process can be personalized to whatever works best for you and your partner.

What's Most Important is Forward Movement

Another byproduct of implementing these changes is that you'll find yourself getting along better with each other. You'll also be less inclined to argue in everyday situations. Family and personal problems will seem less dramatic and difficult to manage. You and your partner—your newfound friend—will want to discuss your relationship situations more frequently and together. The two of you will resolve family and relationship problems more quickly and with less conflict; and compromise will become easier to achieve.

Because of your rejuvenated friendship, you will also discover that you will be happier in your daily activities, and your partner will be affected in a positive way by your new enthusiasm for the relationship. Through it all, you will both grow as individuals and together as a couple, not to mention the closeness and affection that will rekindle the flames of passion that once burned bright in your hearts.

Summary

If you are willing to care enough about yourself and that special person in your life, the possibilities are endless. If you become discouraged, remember you have already separated yourself from most men just because you are willing to accept change. So grab a hug and a kiss from your partner because you have earned it.

Flutter Like a Butterfly

Where a man has a tendency to want to fix a problem, a woman needs to vent. She knows that unloading to just anyone will neither solve the problem nor allow her to calm herself, so her true stress release can only come from her partner.

Here are some tips on how to fine-tune your senses in order to help your partner when she has had a stressful day.

- Because her emotions are already running high it's more important than ever for you to stay grounded and focused on what she needs.

- Do not allow yourself to get caught up in her emotions. Stay calm, cool and collected.
- If she wants to talk about her day, listen to her attentively and sympathetically in a non-judgmental fashion.

Picture a butterfly fluttering around gracefully in a gentle breeze and every so often lands on a flower. Like a butterfly, you need to float around quietly and gently on the fringes of her emotions. You need to give her space if she needs it and support where you can. Give her a few minutes to herself to calm down and relax. Stay patient and content, offering to help out with dinner, doing the laundry or doing something with the kids to allow her time to re-group. You don't want to charge in and say, *"Now what is wrong?"* Take care of her and her needs. Provide her with a little tenderness; give her a smile and a kiss. If you want to earn some brownie points, suggest a shower or a bubble bath and tell her you will take care of the house and look after the kids for a while.

And like a butterfly, fluttering in and out of her emotions and space, check in on her from time to time. Ask her if there is anything you can do for her. She will be happy and thankful for the way that you showed her how much you love her and took care of her.

A man who is wise enough to provide his partner a safe place for her to vent her emotions without criticism or judgment is a man who nurtures a relationship where love and harmony will certainly grow.

The butterfly is considered a symbol of "Divine Love" that represents the human desire to create harmony in life. From the caterpillar stage in the cocoon to the birth of a beautiful, graceful butterfly, it also represents change and growth in an individual.

Can you flutter like a butterfly?

7 | Improving Your Lasting Relationship

> *"The value of a relationship is in direct proportion to the time that you invest in the relationship."*
>
> Brian Tracy

At this point, you should have a clear understanding of how to become best friends with your partner and why doing so is so important. A large part of keeping that friendship alive and flourishing is up to you. Relationships take two, but that doesn't mean the weight is always evenly split 50/50. One of the responsibilities of being a man is going that extra mile at times just to get along. Be proud of your growth process so far. Continue to grow as an individual and together as a couple and your love has an excellent chance of lasting a lifetime.

So, how do you continue to improve your lasting relationship? There are areas that you as the man in the relationship need to pay extra attention to, and then there are those areas that both of you need to focus on.

Remember—where there is love, there is life. Safeguard both of these, nourish them, and keep them healthy.

Staying on the Tightrope

Every relationship has areas that may cause additional stress when they pop up. This section will help you identify those hot areas and give you the tools you need to navigate through them.

Setting Priorities and Realistic Expectations

You need to set priorities from the beginning to help each other understand what to expect in the relationship. Setting priorities has a lot to do with common sense and doing what is right for each person in the relationship, along with the family unit. Your partner and family should always be your first priority.

Realistic expectations within the relationship are just as important as setting priorities and are good for the relationship. They need to be made together and agreeable to both.

Increasing Your Emotional Connection

Creating a strong emotional connection between you and your partner is critical. Having this emotional connection is necessary for you to be able to react to your partner's needs appropriately, and doing so is probably one of the hardest things to recognize in any relationship.

> *An emotional connection is the bonding of two Hearts, Body and Soul moving in the same direction.*

When your partner reaches out to you for emotional comfort she is looking for a hug, a smile, or just a kind word from you. The worst thing you can do is turn away and not respond to her. She is not being needy; she is just looking for your support. Don't you want her to turn to you when she's feeling lost, sad, or upset? Don't you want her to celebrate her happiness with you?

So pay attention to her needs and she will pay attention to yours. By being there for each other, your emotional connection will deepen by making her feel wanted, loved and part of the equation.

The Simple Act of Being Together
Are you there. . . . . Or just in the room?

How often do you actually spend time together? Even if you're both busy people, you need to find a few minutes every day to just be

Improving Your Lasting Relationship

together or to just visit. This is critical so you don't start drifting apart in time.

Here are some ideas to get you started. Some of these will only take a few minutes and can be done spur of the moment, while others will require a little more planning.

- Take a walk in the park, in your neighborhood, or even at the mall on rainy days. Hold hands, talk to each other and enjoy the moment of togetherness. Look around you and feel how special life is and your love for one another. Stop for a few minutes here and there and hug, give her a kiss, slow dance even. This is guaranteed to put a smile on both your faces.
- Find common hobbies or interests you can share together. Take a class together. Visit the museum, the zoo, or anything else that sparks both of your interests.
- Have a date night. Remember when you were first dating and how exciting those dates were—the fireworks, the romance, the excitement of being with each other? Dress up like you used to. Buy her flowers. Plan a special evening out. Get into her heart. Relax, laugh, hold hands, have fun and be romantic. Get goo-goo-eyed with her. Tell her why she is so special. Talk about why you love each other. Celebrate each other and rekindle your romance.
- On a warm evening, sit outside and watch the activity of your neighborhood. Talk to each other about your days, your plans for the future, your friends and family, but mostly, just enjoy the quiet time with each other.
- Cook dinner together. Find a recipe that you both want to try and go shopping together. This can be a great way to spend time with the one you love while turning a normal, everyday task into an adventure. Add a little romance by putting your favorite music on, dancing and singing to each other while cooking in the kitchen.
- If you both love to read, pick out a book and take turns reading out loud to each other. Not only is this fun, it can be extremely

intimate. Curl up on the couch or your bed and get lost in a make believe world together.

There are many other ways you can spend time with your partner, but hopefully these ideas will get you started. Be creative, think about your schedules, and find those moments that are perfect for you and your partner!

Develop Daily Rituals

One of the easiest methods to making your home life more enjoyable and fun is to develop daily rituals with your partner. These can be anything from cooking a meal together, watching a favorite TV show, taking a walk each evening after dinner, riding bikes once a week, visiting the gym together. Anything that allows you to spend time with your partner that can become a daily or weekly part of life is a good thing.

Remember; how you start and end the day will help to build a strong connection with your partner that can keep you (and her) emotionally committed during times of conflict.

One of my favorite rituals or habits is to stay in bed and have a cup of coffee or tea with my partner, talking, laughing, cuddling or making love. This helps me stay grounded and emotionally connected with her.

> **Learn to cherish the moments.**

Taking Care of Each Other

Never forget that one of your jobs as a couple is to take care of one another. If you share a home you share in the financial responsibilities of maintaining and making it a home. Taking care of each other is far more important than money.

Help each other in times of stress or illness. This might mean getting her water in the middle of the night when she has a cold or taking on extra duties at home if she's stuck working a lot of overtime. Take care of the children or play with them so she can have some down time. You want to always look for ways to take care of each other.

When she knows she can count on you, and you know you can count on her, your relationship will strengthen.

Be Courteous

It's important to have faith and trust in your partner. Remember that she loves you until you give her reason not to. If your partner is not accountable, it's difficult to trust them.

For example, not calling home if you're going to be delayed is rude and disrespectful. If hearing from you is important to her, then make sure you contact her. Remember to treat her like you would want to be treated.

Think before you act. Ask yourself this question: "How would I feel if my partner acted in this way?" Would you laugh it off or would you be upset? Chances are it would upset you.

Family Considerations

If the woman in your life is closely involved with her extended family, it will strengthen your relationship if you can accept her family into your heart as your own. Extended families are forever. The last thing you want to do is create dissent between your partner and her family because, trust me, you won't win.

There is literally no easier way to ruin any relationship than to belittle the other person's family. Even if your partner has belittled their own family, you still should not. They have a level of closeness, love, and familiarity that you don't. So they can get away with it. The best advice is to enjoy their family and to learn to accept them.

Outside Friends

Like it or not, you have to share your partner with her friends and vice versa. You can't exactly hide her away in a corner, nor should you even want to.

It is good for everyone to spend social time with friends outside of their romantic relationships. This shouldn't scare you or make you defensive in the least. Remember, you've set boundaries with one another, and they should include having time alone with friends apart from each other.

Be nice and enjoy yourself when she goes out. Put your trust and faith in her unless she gives you a very good reason not to. Be happy when she returns. Ask about her evening and let her know that you missed her. Don't feel as if she's abandoned you for the evening. Besides, if she's happy with her home life, she'll be eager to return home. If she isn't happy, then that's the real issue and it has nothing to do with her being out with her friends. If the latter is an issue, then all the more reason to focus on figuring out why she isn't happy and work through it together.

Outside Obligations

Outside obligations will exist in your relationship, but it's important not to let them get in the way of your family obligations. Your family should always come first.

If an outside obligation interferes with a family obligation, talk to your partner about that obligation. Weigh both sides of the issue, and then decide together what the best course of action is. If you make the decision on your own, and it goes against what your partner wishes and there is then a negative outcome, you might find you've made the wrong decision simply because you didn't have all the necessary facts. By arriving at a decision together, you both become stakeholders of the result of that decision.

I've learned that the smaller your obligation is in your relationship, the less involvement you have in that relationship. In this situation, you and your partner are more likely to drift apart from each other, and if you have children, the end result is even more disastrous.

So, again, communicate with your partner and always put your family first.

Confiding in Others

Sometimes you need to talk to someone other than your partner for advice or a different point of view. This could be a friend, a family member, a co-worker, a member of the clergy, or anyone else that you have trust in. While it's natural to seek out others for advice when there are problems in your relationship, the way you do so is of paramount importance.

- Be sure the person you choose to confide in is a person you can trust implicitly.
- Don't say anything to this person that you wouldn't be willing to say to your partner face-to-face.
- Present the most complete case you can. This means that even if you don't agree with your partner's opinions in the dispute, you should share them as easily as you share yours. That way, your confidant will have all of the facts.
- Let your partner know who you go to for advice and make sure she's comfortable with you talking to that person about relationship issues. For example, she might be completely okay with you talking with your best friend, but not so much if your chosen confidant is her sister.

Furthering Her Education or Career

For whatever reason, some men find it difficult to support their partner's academic and career ambitions. These men tend to feel threatened when the woman in his life wants to further her education or job status. Therefore, he may react negatively, which causes untold strain on the relationship. If you're one of these men, the first step you must take is defining why you feel the way you do.

- Do you feel that you have to be the primary bread winner? If you're not, does it somehow undermine your masculinity?
- Do you need to feel superior to your partner?
- Do you worry that she'll have less time for you?
- Do you worry what your friends are going to say?

It should go without saying that none of these reasons are acceptable, but that doesn't mean they don't matter. Your feelings are important, but in this case, they're wrong. So you need to take some time to think about why you feel insecure or angry, then you need to find a way to support your partner so your relationship won't suffer for it.

It can only benefit you if your woman wants to further her education or improve her employment status. I'm not necessarily talking financially, though that is another likely positive outcome. The best relationships are those with two individuals living the life they want to live with each other. If you put roadblocks in your partner's way, she'll only grow to resent you for doing so.

So, you have two choices: You can either face your own insecurities while supporting your partner, thereby strengthening you and your relationship; or you can undermine her efforts, which can only result in a weakened or fractured relationship. Also, ask yourself if she would support you in such a cause?

The bottom line is that no one should have to justify their decision to further their education and/or career. If there are financial burdens and/or family obligations to consider, then alternatives need to be discussed and compromises arrived at. Remain positive and be proud of her.

Continually Developing Your Relationship

While most of the above points are meant primarily for you, there are other areas in improving your lasting relationship that fall to both you and your partner. It is important that you as a couple have similar goals and values, and you need mutual understanding as to how to achieve them together.

In this section, we'll cover several different areas that both you and your partner need to pay attention to in order to continually develop your relationship.

Communication

When you first met, you started out by creating a friendship and talking. You talked about everything under the sun and spent hours on the phone or on the Internet sending e-mails to one another.

Improving Your Lasting Relationship

So what happened? Why did the two of you stop talking to one another? Why do men feel they don't need to say anything to their partners about what they think or how they feel, but rather keeping their partners at a distance?

Dealing with Disagreements Positively

This chapter wouldn't be complete without giving you some hands-on knowledge on how to deal with disagreements when they arise. After all, no relationship exists in pure harmony. How you handle troubled times is usually far more important than whatever the disagreement is actually about.

We all have little quirks or minor foibles that can irritate our partners. These are not usually a big deal, and shouldn't be unless you make them that way. It is important to put these things in perspective by considering their importance in your life. Are they big enough to address and argue over?

Sometimes it is easier and more sensible to deal with these issues yourself by letting them go and moving on. However, sometimes disagreements happen no matter how hard each person tries to keep the fight at bay. So, if a disagreement is brewing, there are steps you can take to lessen the conflict and eliminate arguing.

Lessening Conflict and Eliminating Arguing

In today's world, conflict is commonplace. You can see it between spouses, friends, co-workers, drivers, parents and children, not to mention entire nations.

In some ways, conflict seems to be acceptable and normal in everyday life. So the key to improving your lasting relationship is to lessen conflict as much as possible and to eliminate arguing. This doesn't mean you can't have disagreements or differences, because you will. What it does mean is that you have to learn to control your emotions during discussions with your partner.

Remember these guidelines:

- Don't lose sight of how much you love and need her in your life.
- Listen with an open mind.

- Don't talk over your partner.
- Understand one another.
- Never raise your voice or speak in anger. If you do, take a deep breath and apologize immediately. You might have to take a timeout and then return to the discussion when you are calmer.
- Don't bring up past situations. You are not keeping score.
- Find the solution or compromise together.

Now, let's take a look at each of these areas in more detail.

Don't Forget How Much You Love Her

If an argument is about to happen, stop yourself and take a few moments to consider your partner's great qualities. Quickly reflect on why you love her, gaze into her eyes and bring back all those amazing feelings. Picture your partner in all her beauty. Your initial burst of anger should lighten, which will put you on neutral ground and should help you regain control of your emotions.

Even if you're a hot-headed individual, there are very few situations that are so important you should get crazy over. Those that do exist, just take them calmly. You can actually train yourself to calm down quickly, so this behavior will become automatic for you.

There are times when keeping your emotions under control may be difficult to say the least. The reason why this is so crucial is if you're over-emotional, you'll have a very difficult time keeping the discussion from escalating into an argument.

Listen With an Open Mind

There can only be one speaker and one listener at a time, so you be the listener first. You have nothing to lose by keeping quiet and paying attention to your partner before she listens to you. It will help you understand exactly where she's coming from when it is your turn to talk.

While she talks, keep the following in mind:

- Why is she upset?
- What is she feeling?

- What is she trying to tell me?
- Why is this important to her?

Listening is done with your ears, eyes and brain, *not* your mouth. Pay attention to her body language, her demeanor, the tone of her voice, and her actions. Try not to formulate any responses until you completely hear her out and understand exactly where she's coming from.

Don't Talk Over Your Partner While She's Talking

One of the first instincts males have is to try to get their point across by talking over their partner or constantly hammering her opinion or point of view. If you find yourself doing this quit immediately. It is a controlling action which will push your partner further away from you in the long run. It is hard to listen if you are the one doing all the talking. Sit back and let her have her say. You might learn something.

Understanding Her Point of View

Understanding your partner's opinions and point of view does not automatically mean you have to agree with her. But understanding why she feels a certain way is crucial.

If a man really wants to understand his partner, he needs to first focus on really knowing her. He needs to know and care about what his partner has been through in her life and how these events have affected her. She is who she is because of her life events. When you understand this, you'll better understand her emotions and her actions.

Pay attention to what is important to her and why. Is she logical or free-willed, constrained or emotional? Understanding the past and how it affects the present not only leads to understanding the present better, but also how it will affect the future.

Never Speak in Anger or Raise Your Voice

Anger and raised voices create a feeling of defensiveness in other people. Therefore, when you raise your voice or speak in anger, you will not only fuel a disagreement into becoming an argument, but you will damage your relationship.

Remember that *mean* words hurt and they can last a lifetime and ruin your relationship. Plus, it's very likely that in a fit of anger, you'll say something you later regret. Unfortunately, you can't turn back the clock and erase unkind words, so stop yourself before saying them.

Raising your voice never solves problems. Rather, it stifles communication and adds to the problem. This will not help you solve anything, and your relationship will suffer for it. Eventually, you'll instill a sickness into your relationship that cannot be cured.

Work to stay calm, understand your partner's feelings the best you can, and then strive for a resolution or a compromise.

Don't Bring Up Past Situations

A lot of people, men and women, tend to "keep score" in their relationships, and bring up past mistakes in current disagreements. Don't do this! The past is over, and that disagreement from three months ago has already been solved, compromised and should be forgotten.

When you toss old grievances into your partner's face, the only result can be negative. Instead, focus on the current discussion and leave old news in the trash where it belongs.

Part of being in a lasting and loving relationship is moving forward. So, keep the past in the past; otherwise you'll add to the confusion and the pain, and make a resolution even harder to reach.

Strengths Over Weaknesses

Everyone has varying amounts of strengths and weaknesses. You and your partner need to find a way to utilize each other's strengths in order to minimize the weaknesses.

If your partner has a great sense of humor, but becomes quiet and withdrawn when something is bothering her, then make her laugh by bringing out that sense of humor to stomp out her withdrawn nature at that moment. Then you can begin the process of communication to find out what's bothering her.

Use the strengths in each other to minimize the weaknesses and not only will your relationship grow stronger, but increased trust will develop, which will increase your emotional connection to each other.

Find the Solution or Compromise Together

Finding the appropriate solution or compromise together isn't always easy, but it is doable. There should be no issues that you and your partner cannot find a resolution or compromise for that appeal to both of you.

Here are some pointers:

- Talk the issue over calmly, each taking turns listening, sharing, and responding.
- Remember to smile and show your love and support.
- If things begin to go south, take a quick break, and then when you come back together, remind her that this is something you're working on together as a team.
- Be aware of and accept the problem(s) as fact, at least from your partner's point of view.
- Calmly discuss various possibilities for resolution and/or compromises until you both are satisfied with the result.
- Hug each other and celebrate the accomplishment of reaching the end of a disagreement in a positive manner.

She's Special — So Remind Her

There are so many ways you can remind your partner that she's special.

- Send her flowers at work.
- Surprise her with a card and/or a small gift.
- Call her in the middle of the day and tell her you love her.
- Give her an impromptu kiss when she's least expecting it.
- Tell her she's beautiful.

Summary

Your relationship can and should continue to evolve. You and your partner should never lose the ground you've already covered, and should be continually moving forward. By using the information in this chapter, you'll be creating a relationship that will last a lifetime, one in which both of you will find joy, love, and ongoing support. Always remember:

- Your partner is your best friend. Treat her as such with love, respect, honesty, and care.
- Take time every day to spend time with your significant other, even if it's just for a few minutes. Those moments add up.
- Keep communication open and ongoing.
- Work daily to minimize conflict and when there is a disagreement, show your patience, love, and willingness to understand her side.

Nurturing a relationship is akin to keeping a garden alive by removing the weeds. Neglect will kill the love between you and your partner as quickly as ignoring your garden will kill your plants. Keep your love alive and your relationship will always be in bloom.

You are my Life ... Now and Forever
No matter what life brings us
We can withstand the test of time

Together as One
Sharing in every heartbeat
Every breath we take

I love our life we share in
The world we are creating together

With you holding my hand
There is nothing we can't do or accomplish together
You complement me in every way
And complete my world

Together in Love
Forever and a Day

8 | The Importance of Physical Contact

"Passion is the quickest to develop, and the quickest to fade. Intimacy develops more slowly, and commitment more gradually still."

Robert Sternberg

Intimacy is not just about sex. It is about closeness and being with your partner. It's about becoming one breath and one soul. It is about merging two hearts into one heartbeat. Intimacy can be as simple as holding each other close and talking. It is as critical to your relationship as oxygen is to your life, for without it, your relationship will smother and die or become stagnant.

Intimacy takes many forms and there is no end of fun things that you and your partner can do together. Here are a few easy ideas to get the fire burning:

- Sing a love song to her. It really doesn't matter if you sing off-key. Trust me; she will love you for trying it.
- Dance together in the house or dance for each other. Light some candles and find some romantic music on the radio or CD.
- Try feeding your partner; it can be so silly, fun and enjoyable.
- Take a shower or bubble bath together and gently lather or wash each other. Wash her hands and feet, and let her wash yours. This can be very erotic.
- Hugging, kissing, and just playing together are great expressions of intimacy.

- Do chores together. Share the same sink in the bathroom, and talk to each other while doing so.
- Serve her breakfast in bed as her personal chef. Even if you burn the toast, she won't complain. But try not to set the kitchen on fire in the process. And don't forget about dessert!
- Surprise her with a gift or a romantic card, "just because you love her". Put it where she will find it later—in her purse, on her pillow or in the bathroom.
- Have a romantic dinner by candlelight with a long stemmed rose at her place setting.
- If she likes romantic novels, read one out loud to her, but don't laugh unless it's really meant to be funny. You might be surprised by what a turn-on it is for both of you.

Intimacy in Your Relationship

With the above in mind, let's take a closer look at ways you can increase the level of intimacy with your partner.

> **Set the Mood of Romance for life!**

Physical Affection

Humans need to touch and to be touched. Remember as a child how good it felt when you were hugged? You knew you were loved, and you felt safe. As much fuss as we make about personal space, infants and children are not the only ones who need regular physical contact; we all do.

Perhaps it is hard-wired from evolutionary biology, but many women seem to need physical touch more than men do. That's not to say that men don't need physical touch, but women speak a different "physical language" than men do and appreciate different types of physical affection.

Think about all the ways you can add the sensation of touching into your relationship. Hold hands while you walk, watch TV or cuddle in bed. Lean across the kitchen table to give her a quick kiss or to stroke her cheek. Give a gentle kiss on her neck while cooking and give her a quick squeeze.

Physical contact can communicate as much as verbal language. It can tell the other person that the relationship is safe, loving, comforting, playful, and respectful—all without saying a word. Your partner is unconsciously reading and processing every gesture and expression you make. One's tone of voice and accompanying expressions/gestures often resonates significantly more than what we actually say.

If, however, your partner is having an off day, doesn't feel well, or for whatever reason isn't in the mood to be touched at that moment, respect her space and find other ways to show her you care.

Embrace: The Power of a Hug

An embrace is shared among parent and child, friends, and significant others. It is a universal expression of friendship used for comfort, forgiveness, acceptance, welcome, and many other purposes. You can communicate all of this and more to your partner simply by giving her a hug.

When you embrace her, you show her that you love her unconditionally, protect her from the world and comfort her when she is hurting. Welcome her when she comes home for work, forgive her any transgressions against you, and accept her for who she is. When you let her embrace you, you allow her to do the same for you. And if the hug is present throughout your relationship, it will be all the more meaningful and comforting when it is needed the most, such as when a loved one passes, a job is lost, or a dream is shattered. Embracing your partner often and with passion should be the "physical affection" foundation.

The Art of the Kiss

Do you remember the excitement and anticipation of your very first kiss? How long were you planning the perfect backdrop in your head? Days? Weeks? Months? Your heart was probably racing and you forgot to breathe.

Are your current thoughts about kissing her dramatically different now? To a certain extent, that's to be expected. After years, even decades, kissing tends to lose its uniqueness. But kissing is an important way to show affection in your relationship. To many woman, kisses are the most important and enjoyable aspects of a relationship. The first kiss is the strongest memory she has from the beginning of your relationship and one she'll carry in her heart forever.

She'll never forget the magical power of your first Kiss

Sadly, after many years in a relationship, kisses become sort of cookie-cutter and mechanical. If kissing has become a boring activity without any diversity, it's time to heat things up. Think of all of the different adjectives that might describe a kiss: passionate, sloppy, soft, sensual, long and playful. Choose a random day and kiss your partner passionately for a minimum of 15 seconds, slowly pulling away. Can you feel the excitement?

Some of the most passionate kisses are the ones not necessarily placed on the lips. Kisses on the neck, arms, back, even feet can send tingles throughout her body. If you feel like having fun, before you kiss your partner, have her close her eyes and you choose where and what the kiss will be like. This guarantees that the "cookie-cutter" kiss will make way for a much more exciting version of itself. You can even make a game of this with your partner. Take turns. Have fun and enjoy each other.

A Little Cuddle Time

Cuddling is not a three-letter word—meaning *SEX*. After all, children love being close to their security blankets. Infants do well when they hear their mother's heartbeat.

I'm not sure why many men cringe when they hear the word "cuddle", possibly because television and movies have turned it into a feminine thing.

Cuddling makes you very aware of the presence of your partner— the feel of her skin, her hair, her scent—things that we may not fully appreciate in the hustle and bustle of daily life. Spend time embracing, talking, laughing, hugging, and kissing before going to sleep. Learn to enjoy your downtime together.

Always remember to kiss her first thing in the morning and last thing at night before you go to sleep. The security and comfort we feel when we are physically close to another person makes it easier for us to let down our emotional guard and share our hearts with our partners.

Massaging Out the Kinks

Massaging can work out muscle kinks, but it can also work out some of the kinks in your relationship. If you had two choices: to be stressed or to be relaxed, which would you choose? The answer is pretty obvious. No one wants to feel tension or pain. One of the easiest, selfless things you can do for your partner is to give her a massage without the expectation of a massage in return.

How grateful would you be to someone who was able to lessen or reduce pain that you were experiencing? Giving a full-body massage can help you locate your partner's hot button areas. Adding oils, lotions, candles, and music will create a wonderfully romantic environment.

A massage can also be given when clothes are on. While a massage can be a great way of developing intimacy and can be effective foreplay, it should not be used solely with the expectation of sex. She will be more appreciative if she doesn't suspect you of having an ulterior motive. And, by showing her you care, you'll not only alleviate any physical stress she might be feeling, but emotional stress, as well.

Foreplay vs. Sex

Men seem to lose sight of this very important step in the physical process when they are in sight of their own goal of sex or self-gratification. Imagine if someone told you that you could only have sex ONE more time in your life. I bet you would take your time loving your partner, making it last as long as possible. Foreplay is the sizzle to a great steak. Spending time kissing and touching each other is what creates that excitement, and those feelings are important to your partner. If you are doing it right you should be bonding together as one soul and body.

Great sex is important in your relationship. The next time you're in the heat of the moment, take your time pleasing her. Have fun and enjoy each other's company. Remember: *foreplay is eight letters, while sex is only three.* Therefore, foreplay should last longer than sex.

I truly believe that the basis for great lovemaking is the friendship that grows between two partners. Romance, love, respect, loyalty and communication while pleasing your partner comes naturally. I think that lovemaking between two people should be that bond that truly makes them one with each other, that sets them apart from everyone else. There are no boundaries when it comes to pleasing your partner. I hope that I will be making love to my partner until I am 90!

Appreciation as a Form of Intimacy

Showing appreciation for your partner should be done whenever you think of it, at any moment during the day, and can be done in many different ways. At least one day per month do something special together. Leave the kids at home and just the two of you go out for dinner or take in a movie.

If you can afford it, go to a fancy Spa Hotel or Bed and Breakfast Inn and stay in a room with a king-sized bed and a Jacuzzi in the room. Take a shower together with music and candlelight, and then order room service. Use that time to rejuvenate your friendship and your love for each other. It will be a night you will both remember and cherish forever.

Take your camera with you wherever you go, not just on vacations. Take memorable, romantic photos for each other as well as have people take photos of you as a couple. Take funny pictures of each other around the house. Then make a photo album together of some of your favorite places. These memories will continually reinforce your love for each other and bring both of you closer together.

Create a Keepsake Box

A keepsake box contains the snapshots of the events and little things you do together as a couple. Your keepsake box could be a big shoebox or a fancy hatbox, any kind of container. What makes this keepsake box so special is what you keep inside it—those precious reminders of the things you have done together—a treasure chest of your warm-hearted memories.

Your keepsake box can consist of special cards, dried flowers, ticket stubs, a seashell, a special heart-shaped rock, special events, a napkin you wrote on, a ribbon, or other mementos of places you've collected together through the years. Write the date with an inscription on some of your items of what you did and where you were that made that day so special. At least once a year pull out your keepsake box and go through it together.

A keepsake box is a thoughtful gift for her, for no other reason than to say "I Love You", and will reap untold benefits. When you show your partner you appreciate her you'll increase the bonds of intimacy within your relationship.

Take a Cruise Ship Excursion

Taking a cruise was one of the most memorable, romantic experiences of my life. I can't think of a better way to rejuvenate a relationship or strengthen family ties. As I sat around the pool, I noticed couples of all ages enjoying each other. The families with children were having a ball. There was laughter everywhere.

The atmosphere is relaxing, romantic and uplifting with tropical drinks reminiscent of a honeymoon. It is a wonderful way to rekindle your relationship.

The views from the decks are spectacular and breathtaking. Nighttime on a cruise ship is incredible, the way the moon glistens and sparkles off of the water. The stars appear so bright and close; you feel like you could reach out and touch them. If you didn't feel like going out for the evening, you could snuggle up in your bed, get lost in each other's arms and order room service.

If you feel like adventure, you have a choice of some unbelievable exotic locations, excursions and sightseeing. The list of fun and romantic things you can share are without limit: theatre, comedy clubs, karaoke nights, dining, dancing, parties, gambling and swimming. Romance is everywhere and within an easy reach.

Summary

Your relationship with your partner is unique. Therefore, how you choose to increase your intimacy will likely differ from other couples. But, the main ingredients are the same for every couple. You know your partner better than anyone else, so you should be able to discern what matters to her the most.

Does she dislike public displays of affection? If so, you probably don't want to kiss her in public, but instead holding hands may be a good compromise. Or maybe she doesn't like being kissed or touched before she has her first cup of coffee in the morning. If you know this, you should follow her lead.

All of the examples in this chapter are sound, but you should fine-tune them to fit your relationship and your partner.

Remember, intimacy is as crucial to your relationship as oxygen is to your life. Increasing the bonds of intimacy with your partner can only result in a positive outcome.

Conclusion: My Last Bit of Advice

"Love at first sight is easy to understand; it's when two people have been looking at each other for a lifetime that it becomes a miracle."

Amy Bloom

CONGRATULATIONS! You made it! This is definitely a major accomplishment and you should feel terrific about it. Pat yourself on the back and grab a hug from your partner for committing yourself to read this book, and loving her enough to make your life together better.

I sincerely hope that my thoughts within the prior pages stay with you as you go about your daily life with your partner.

Before I conclude, I have one last analogy I'd like to share for making your relationship work.

Tune Up Your Relationship

Relationships take on a life of their own, and like with most things in life they require maintenance. If we don't maintain them, sometimes they can become stagnant or unexciting.

Every car needs regular tune-ups to run more efficiently and effectively. We accept this without question or protest. We check the tires, oil and fluid levels, wash it and take care of it, regardless of the make, model or year. Car care takes some planning and scheduling, but we do it, and we usually keep them for only a few years.

Yet, in our most important personal relationships, we don't think to check for problems or even notice the warning lights that may indicate that something might be wrong. Most guys operate as though being a friend to their lover isn't necessary or important.

We typically take a cynical view of self-help books on relationships. We'll take our car in to keep it running smoothly and elongate its life, but practicing friendship, communication, intimacy, compassion, understanding, and patience is another issue altogether. *So be the mechanic of your family.* Put on your coveralls. Grab your toolbox and get to work.

Consider this book your manual for a smoother-running relationship as seen through the eyes of an "Average Bruce."

I've written this book based on my personal growth and my own experiences, so I realize every experience may not be like yours. But, I've spoken to plenty of men and women who recognize more than just a few things in this book that would enhance the quality of their relationship with their partner.

You will undoubtedly have to put forth some effort in order to see some improvement and the amount and quality of your effort is directly proportional to an enhanced, more exciting relationship.

As you apply the principles you have learned in this book it is likely that you'll begin to notice a significant improvement in your relationship. As your partner feels the new, regenerated love you are sharing with her, she cannot help but want to grow right along with you. All those little arguments and conflicts will slowly start to dissipate and eventually disappear. You will begin to be more aware of your words and actions, and be as concerned about her well-being as you are yours. That's the true meaning of love.

Make a commitment to yourself and your partner that you will make this work. Don't worry about making mistakes. You're allowed to stumble and fall. That is a part of the learning and growing process. Don't get discouraged. Don't constantly try to be perfect or compare yourself to any other person. Stay true to yourself. Just keep trying to avoid the mistakes that you made yesterday. Keep learning to be more aware of the things you do and say and appreciate your own

Conclusion: My Last Bit of Advice

progress. Your partner, and now your new best friend, will too. You'll find yourself wanting to be together more often, just like best friends as you watch your love blossom.

I'd love to hear how your newfound energy has improved your relationship. Please send me your positive feedback and your success stories. Keep me posted on your progress at my Web site, www.LuvIsForever.com. I'll be happy to keep in touch. And if you've enjoyed this book, please encourage other couples to read it.

I hope my book has given you a new perspective on how to view life and the relationship you share. If you were able to obtain or use at least one idea from my book, I feel that I've accomplished my goal ...

> **TO CHANGE THE WORLD.... ONE COUPLE AT A TIME**

Good luck, and know that I'm wishing you and your relationship the very best.

Bonus Section: Women Love Poetry

"Poetry is the universal language which the heart holds with nature and itself."

William Hazlitt

Women love poetry, but even more importantly, they love it when a man can communicate in a romantic, sentimental way. Written and spoken words have an everlasting effect on your relationship. Writing poetry doesn't have to be that difficult. Don't say you can't unless you try.

Writing poetry is a sure way of getting brownie points with your partner, and it doesn't make you any less manly, either. After all, most poet laureates have been men.

Here are some quick pointers on how to write poetry:

- The key to writing poetry is that every word and the sentiment you're expressing have to come from your heart.
- Say what you feel.
- Write with passion.
- Let yourself go.
- It doesn't matter if it rhymes and there are no requirements for length.

So, if you want to give writing poetry a try, write three or four sentences or a paragraph of what you want to say. Take the last word of each odd numbered sentence and try to rhyme them. Not every other line or lines have to rhyme. Just try to make it follow evenly. There is no right or wrong way to write poetry.

Just as writing poetry is important, how you share the poems with your partner is just as critical. Be creative when presenting them to her. Leave one on her pillow for her to find. Hide a card with a few poetic lines in her purse to find at work. Giving her something sweet and simple on a card will make a lasting impression.

Romance Is ...

Romance isn't just a birthday, anniversary or a special occasion. Romance is a way of life. Romance is loving her every hour of every day, appreciating her every minute along the way, and telling her about it. Romance is a look, a hug, a kiss out of nowhere. Saying "I Love You," just because you are there.

Here is a little poem to help understand how magical romance should be:

Romance is ... sharing each other's heartbeat and breath
Romance is ... a way of kissing without touching
Romance is ... feeling each other's hugs when you are miles apart
Romance is ... tenderness and softness, a look, a touch, a smile
Romance is ... wanting to be together every moment to share—to care—to trust
Romance is ... strength and power ... a feeling ... a desire ... an answer
Romance is many little things in life
But most of all ...
Romance is ...
Loving her
The best way you know how

MY SOULMATE

S — Strength, Sensitive, Sensual, Stunning, Sweet, Sensational, Sunshine

O — Open, Overpowering, Only One

U — Unselfish, Understanding

L — Loving, Lasting, Lady

M — Magical, Magnificent, Mesmerizing, Magnetic

A — Affectionate, Adoring, Appreciate

T — Trusting, Tender, Thoughtful, Tantalizing

E — Elegant, Enticing, Exquisite Enchanting, Everlasting

Afterthought

Think back to when you were first dating or the first year of your relationship. It was awesome. The fireworks were flying and you couldn't handle not being near each other for any length of time. Remember when you really missed each other? Wouldn't you like it to be that way again? Well, it can be.

Two growing individuals make up a growing relationship. A growing relationship will always find a way to stay happy. Hopefully you will want to change and improve as you become more aware of your lesser contributions within your relationship. As you create a stronger *friendship* with your partner, you will automatically start to grow as an individual and your partner will grow right along with you.

> **Friendship is the Beauty of a Lasting Relationship.**

Bonus Section: Women Love Poetry

Here are extra charts of A and B for you and your partner to use. As before, rate yourself in each of the following categories on a scale between 1 and 5, with 1 needing the greatest improvement and 5 meaning that particular trait is mastered or does not currently need attention. Be sure to circle whether you're willing to work on any of these traits or not. There are spaces for you to fill in other traits you feel are important.

After you have completed filling out *Chart B* with your partner, compare your answers. This might feel a little awkward or difficult, but it's an essential step that shouldn't be skipped. Remember: it is critical to know how other people perceive you, especially the person with whom you are in a relationship. Then average your score with your partner's into one number in the last column. For example, if you have a "3" in one area, and your partner gave you a "1" on the same trait, then the average score would be a "2." Do this for every trait and every score.

Chart A: Personal Traits

TRAIT	SELF-ASSESSMENT	WILL WORK ON?
Communication	1 2 3 4 5	YES NO
Listening	1 2 3 4 5	YES NO
Respect	1 2 3 4 5	YES NO
Self-Confidence	1 2 3 4 5	YES NO
Sense of Humor	1 2 3 4 5	YES NO
Positive Attitude/Outlook	1 2 3 4 5	YES NO
Honesty	1 2 3 4 5	YES NO
Trustworthy	1 2 3 4 5	YES NO
Compassion	1 2 3 4 5	YES NO
Thoughtfulness/Caring	1 2 3 4 5	YES NO
Desire for Growth	1 2 3 4 5	YES NO
Patience	1 2 3 4 5	YES NO
Open-Mindedness	1 2 3 4 5	YES NO
Word Choices	1 2 3 4 5	YES NO
	1 2 3 4 5	YES NO
	1 2 3 4 5	YES NO
	1 2 3 4 5	YES NO

Chart B: Assessment of Your Traits Within Your Relationship

Trait	Self	Partner	Average
Communication			
Discussing your feelings and problems.	1 2 3 4 5	1 2 3 4 5	1 2 3 4 5
Explaining clearly your wants and desires.	1 2 3 4 5	1 2 3 4 5	1 2 3 4 5
Not raising your voice or yelling.	1 2 3 4 5	1 2 3 4 5	1 2 3 4 5
Repeating questions or statements (nagging).	1 2 3 4 5	1 2 3 4 5	1 2 3 4 5
Carefully choosing words that are constructive.	1 2 3 4 5	1 2 3 4 5	1 2 3 4 5
Positive reinforcement.	1 2 3 4 5	1 2 3 4 5	1 2 3 4 5
Listening			
Allowing your partner to express her opinion.	1 2 3 4 5	1 2 3 4 5	1 2 3 4 5
Taking interest in what your partner says.	1 2 3 4 5	1 2 3 4 5	1 2 3 4 5
Acknowledging that you understand what your partner says.	1 2 3 4 5	1 2 3 4 5	1 2 3 4 5
Open-Minded			
Nonjudgmental	1 2 3 4 5	1 2 3 4 5	1 2 3 4 5
Opinionated	1 2 3 4 5	1 2 3 4 5	1 2 3 4 5
Willing to look at issues from another person's perspectives.	1 2 3 4 5	1 2 3 4 5	1 2 3 4 5
Open to self-improvement.	1 2 3 4 5	1 2 3 4 5	1 2 3 4 5

Trait	Self	Partner	Average
Problem Resolution			
Willing to discuss problems openly.	1 2 3 4 5	1 2 3 4 5	1 2 3 4 5
Taking responsibility for your part of the issue.	1 2 3 4 5	1 2 3 4 5	1 2 3 4 5
Willing to take action to resolve problems.	1 2 3 4 5	1 2 3 4 5	1 2 3 4 5
Maintaining the resolution.	1 2 3 4 5	1 2 3 4 5	1 2 3 4 5

Bonus Section: Women Love Poetry

Trait	Self	Partner	Average
Confidence			
Jealousy	1 2 3 4 5	1 2 3 4 5	1 2 3 4 5
Trust in your partner.	1 2 3 4 5	1 2 3 4 5	1 2 3 4 5
Attitude			
Controlling and/or dominating	1 2 3 4 5	1 2 3 4 5	1 2 3 4 5
Ego	1 2 3 4 5	1 2 3 4 5	1 2 3 4 5
Stubbornness	1 2 3 4 5	1 2 3 4 5	1 2 3 4 5
Honesty	1 2 3 4 5	1 2 3 4 5	1 2 3 4 5
Positive behavior	1 2 3 4 5	1 2 3 4 5	1 2 3 4 5
Thoughtfulness	1 2 3 4 5	1 2 3 4 5	1 2 3 4 5
Caring	1 2 3 4 5	1 2 3 4 5	1 2 3 4 5
Affectionate	1 2 3 4 5	1 2 3 4 5	1 2 3 4 5
Courtesy (Opening doors, etc.)	1 2 3 4 5	1 2 3 4 5	1 2 3 4 5
Patient	1 2 3 4 5	1 2 3 4 5	1 2 3 4 5
Attentive	1 2 3 4 5	1 2 3 4 5	1 2 3 4 5

Trait	Self	Partner	Average
Sharing Household Duties			
Laundry	1 2 3 4 5	1 2 3 4 5	1 2 3 4 5
Cleaning	1 2 3 4 5	1 2 3 4 5	1 2 3 4 5
Dishes	1 2 3 4 5	1 2 3 4 5	1 2 3 4 5
Grocery shopping	1 2 3 4 5	1 2 3 4 5	1 2 3 4 5
Helping with the kids	1 2 3 4 5	1 2 3 4 5	1 2 3 4 5
Respect			
Criticizing	1 2 3 4 5	1 2 3 4 5	1 2 3 4 5
Respect partner's feelings.	1 2 3 4 5	1 2 3 4 5	1 2 3 4 5
Respect partner's opinions.	1 2 3 4 5	1 2 3 4 5	1 2 3 4 5
Appearance			
Hygiene	1 2 3 4 5	1 2 3 4 5	1 2 3 4 5
Fitness	1 2 3 4 5	1 2 3 4 5	1 2 3 4 5

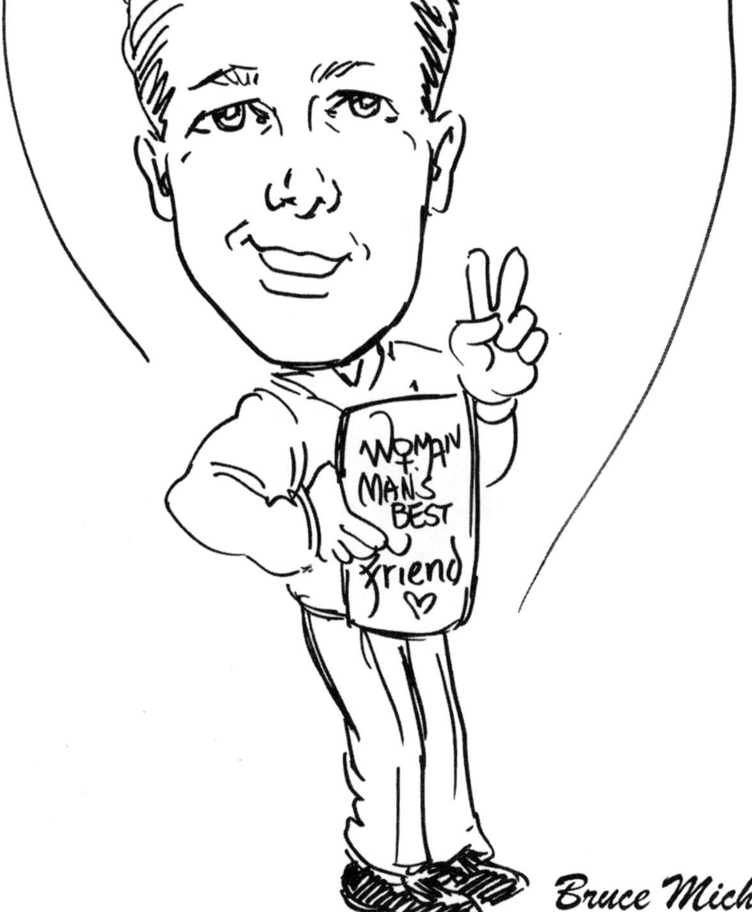

Bruce Michaels